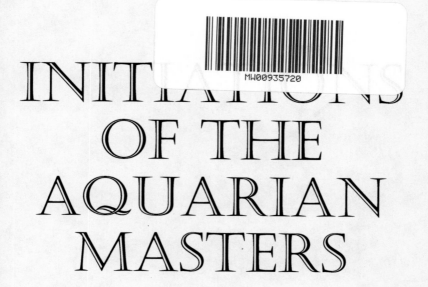

INITIATIONS OF THE AQUARIAN MASTERS

JACOB L. WATSON, III, D.D.

THE THEOSOPHY OF THE AQUARIAN GOSPEL

Outskirts Press, Inc.
Denver, Colorado

Outskirts Press, Inc.
http://www.outskirtspress.com

ISBN: 978-1-4327-4598-1

Outskirts Press and the "OP" logo are trademarks belonging to Outskirts Press, Inc.

PRINTED IN THE UNITED STATES OF AMERICA

Contents

Abbreviations

AG - *Aquarian Gospel of Jesus the Christ*
Biopneuma - *Biopneuma: The Science of the Great Breath by Levi H. Dowling*
KJV - *King James Version of the Holy Bible*
NEB - *New English Version of the Holy Bible*
SC - *Self-Culture by Levi H. Dowling*

Illumination by Levi

There's an ocean that men cannot fathom
nor measure;
It lies just beyond the Dominion of Night;
'Tis the ocean of splendor, of infinite pleasure,
Of fathomless beauty - the ocean of Light.

In the midst of this radiant ocean of glory
Rests the Island of Blessing, the gem of the sea;
The home of the Spirit, so famous in story,
Where angels are servants, and men are the free.

In the midst of the Isle is a flower-crowned mountain;
The sanctified call it the Mount of the Wise;
From its summit pours forth a life-giving fountain
That waters the lands of the earth and the skies.

On top of the mountain a Temple, all glorious,
Stand out in the light of the illumined One.
Ten thousand bright angels and souls all victorious,
Surround it, and fill it - this House of the Sun.

And this is the Temple of Illumination

Where the courtiers of heaven and earth daily meet;
Where souls, cleansed from sin,
elect from each nation,
Hold council with Jesus, and sit at his feet.

The way to this Island and unto this Mountain
Lies through the deep valley of Silence and Prayer;
But whoever will may drink from the Fountain,
And realize all that it is to be there.

Come up to this Temple of Illumination;
Come, bathe in the sunlight of a thrice blessed day.
There is room for the millions of every nation,
And Christ is the Truth and the Life and the Way.

In the innermost Circle there's joy
and there's gladness;
There's peace and there's freedom
from sin and from strife.
The Angel of Mercy will free you from sadness,
And Christ's Benediction is Eternal Life.

by Levi from *Biopneuma*

Formula of the Seeker
Wisdom! Wisdom! Wisdom!
It must be mine;

Light! Light! Light!
I will see the True Light;
Illumination! Illumination! Illumination!
I will attain unto Divine Illumination,
Though Jesus Christ, My Lord.

by Levi from Biopneuma, Pg. 56

The Mercy Seat
There is a place where Spirits blend,
Where friend holds fellowship with friend.
Though sundered far by faith they meet
Around one common Mercy Seat.

by Levi from *Biopneuma*, Pg. 37

Forward: An Invitation

This volume is given for the benefit of those seekers of the Truth, those who desire to possess the Kingdom of Heaven and the Aquarian Christine Church, Universal, Inc.. It is the fruit of a lifetime of study and is presented in as simple a manner as possible. It is the whole hearted, loving desire of the author at this Dawning of the Age of Aquarius, the Spirit Age, to bring reform and greater clarity. So much information under the guise of "New Age" is of suspect character and full of human misconception, folly and strong egos desiring personal glorification. Entities channeled through obsessed and possessed individuals are sadly swaying corruptible and gullible individuals. Yes, a great reform is needed to purify the Teachings of the Ascended Masters of the Silent Brotherhood.

The Aquarian Christine Church, Universal, Inc. is open to all who are sincerely interested. We do not ask others to convert or stop attending other religious meetings. We have no requirements for membership. We do not require tithes, but do accept monetary offerings given in faith and love. Although we are not opposed to rites such as baptism and communion, like other faiths, such as the Salvation Army and the Society of Friends (Quakers), we have found that in the Light of God, we worship in Spirit and need no outward physical rituals.

Silence is golden. Silent prayer is practiced at services and is considered direct communion with God, the God that lives within your heart. Spoken prayer and music are also featured.

I. Introduction

The Aquarian Christine Church Universal, Inc. was incorporated Pentecost Sunday (Whitsunday) 2006. Members are commonly called Aquarians, but the proper term is Christines. Sometimes the church is commonly called the Aquarian Church. The Church is based on The Aquarian Gospel of Jesus the Christ, a work of holy scripture transcribed by Levi H. Dowling from the Akashic Records, the Book of Life, which is the etheric records of everything forming the Book of God's Remembrance. Levi transcribed The AG in the Presence of God Almighty before God's Throne in the Highest Realm of Heaven. The AG was copyrighted in 1907 and published in 1908. It is the story of Jesus the Christ's whole life, including the missing years not recorded in the New Testament and much, much more. During these missing years from ages 13 to around 29, Jesus journeyed through parts of the modern countries of Iraq, Iran, Afghanistan, Pakistan, India, Tibet, Greece and Egypt. It is the message from God for the Age of Aquarius, it is new and modern, yet it is also ancient. The AG proclaims the Return of Christ during the Age of Aquarius and the transformation of the Earth into Paradise - Heaven on Earth. All who embrace the Mighty Truth of The AG are Aquarian Christines.

During the travels of Jesus, He studied the scriptures, teachings and philosophies from the greatest Masters of the revealed religions of the World at that time which included: Greek Philosophy and Religion, Judaism, Egyptian Religion, Zoroastrianism, Hinduism, Buddhism and Taoism. Jesus also was an outspoken teacher and reformer of all of these religions and philosophies and was often feared, hated, rejected, and his murder plotted. *The AG* asserts that Jesus Christ is **the fulfiller of all revealed religions**. He did not come only to reform Judaism, but **all world religion**. Therefore, Aquarian Christines feel the Christian dispensation to be of the highest of all religions, before the more thoroughly revealed Aquarian Christine Church Universal, Inc. came into being.

'The Christine Church is but the kingdom of the Holy One within the soul, made manifest.

The Christine Lord has sent us forth to open up the gates of dawn. Through Christ all men may enter into light and life.

The Christine Church stands on the postulates that Jesus is the love of God made manifest; that love is savior of the sons of men.' - *AG* 182: 33-35

There are some mysteriously uncovered, hidden

2

Buddhist scriptures that are considered sacred on a level only slightly less than *The AG,* which are: *The Life of Saint Issa* uncovered by Nicholas Notovich; and *Jesus Christ, the Leader of Men* from the Himis manuscript translated by Swami Abhedananda. These discovered scriptures support the authenticity of *The AG.*

The Christine Church has many unique beliefs that surprisingly appeals to those who do not care for traditional organized religions. Some beliefs include: the Goal of the Perfection of the Self (Body, Soul and Spirit); the Imminent Spiritual Return of Christ during the Age of Aquarius; Reincarnation and the Liberation from Karma and Reincarnation by the Reality of the Resurrection and Ascension Processes; Simple Sacred Rites and the Freedom from all Ritual known as Inner Light; the femininity of the Holy Spirit; the Elohim, Seraphim, Cherubim, Archangels, Angels, Elemental Spirits, and Ascended Masters; the power to command elemental spirits and to vanquish demonic and disembodied souls and spirits; the potential of everyone to become Divine through Christ Consciousness - everyone is a potential Christ and Ascended Master.

The Christine Church believes in the literal meaning of the Priesthood of All Believers. In contrast to most religions, everyone is a Priest or Priestess in their own temple of their Body, Soul and Spirit. Therefore, there is no laity, everyone is clergy and may be a legally ordained minister or not. This is why we do not try to convert or proselytize, because everyone is clergy, we consider it a calling. Every member is a king or queen in the Royal Priesthood of the Kingdom of Heaven, Christ is the High Priest of Priests and King of Kings, we are His servants. He is the Shepherd, we are the sheep. He is the Bridegroom, the Christine Church and the Kingdom of Heaven is the Bride of Christ - "Christine." There is no paid clergy and any member of the Church may take part in all phases of the services, except perform weddings, which have to have a legally ordained minister or rather have a document that proves that one is clergy.

The Aquarian Christine Church teaches complete equality of all human beings and does not discriminate against anyone in its membership, but does reserve the rights to screen potential members and refuse membership. All property, presentations, meetings and services of the church are private and not considered open to the public.

The Priesthood

'When man sees God as one with him, as Father-God, he needs no middle man, no priest to intercede; He goes straight up to him and says, My Father-God! And then he lays his hand in God's own hand, and all is well.
And this is God. You are, each one, a priest, just for yourself...' - *AG* 28: 22-24

Prayer of Justice

My Father-God, Who was, and is, and evermore
shall be;
Who holds within Thy Hands the scales of Justice
and Right.
Who in Thy Boundless Love has made all men to
equal be.
The black, the yellow, the red and the white;
Can look up in Thy face and say, Our Father-God.
Thou Father of the human race,
Thy name I praise. - *AG* 24

II. Levi

Levi H. Dowling was born May 18th, 1844 in Belleville, Ohio. His father was a pioneer and Disciples of Christ preacher/minister. As a young boy Levi was aware of and highly sensitized to the finer etheric realm, he felt that there are etheric vibrations underlying all sounds, thoughts and events that are recorded on sensitized etheric plates (something like a Divine Computer disk). During his childhood he was an avid student of all of the world's religions. Also, when just a lad he had a vision in which he was told he was to "build a white city." The vision was repeated three more times over the years; the building of the "white city" was his transcribing of The Aquarian Gospel of Jesus the Christ.

When Levi was only thirteen years old he debated a Presbyterian elder on the doctrine of everlasting damnation and torment of souls in Hell. At a very early age Levi understood the Truth that the doctrine of eternal damnation is incompatible with a Just, Loving and Forgiving God of Infinite Mercy. At an early age Levi was a prophet and seer of God's Word. At sixteen, following in his father's footsteps, Levi was a preacher; at eighteen he was pastor of a small church.

During the Civil War (1861-1865), Levi was a chaplain in the U.S. Army and delivered President Lincoln's eulogy at his memorial services for the Union forces in Illinois. After the war, Levi attended Northwestern Christian University at Indianapolis, Indiana and was the graduate of two medical colleges. He practiced medicine for many years and taught the use of electricity to medical students, demonstrating that he was a pioneer of modern medicine. He also worked for the cause of the Prohibition of alcohol, although the use of alcohol is not forbidden by *The AG*, its abuse is highly discouraged. Levi passed from
earth-life August 13, 1911, he is now an Ascended Master.

For forty years Levi studied and meditated upon mysteries in quiet contemplation until he reached such a level of spiritual consciousness he entered Akasha and stood before the Very Throne of God. There Visel Goddess of Wisdom, the Holy Breath (the Holy Spirit), the Mother God spoke unto Levi and gave him his commission to transcribe The AG of Jesus the Christ. This is recorded in the beginning chapters of *The AG* in the section called *Levi's Commission*. Here are some excerpts:

'And then Visel the holy one stood forth and said:

O, Levi, son of man, behold, for you are called to be

the message bearer of the coming age - the age of Spirit blessedness.

Behold the Akasha! Behold the Record Galleries of Visel where every thought and word and deed of every living thing is written down.

Now, Levi, hearken to my words: go forth into these mystic Galleries and read. There you will find a message for the world; for every man; for every living thing.

I breathe upon you now the Holy Breath; you will discriminate, and you will know the lessons that these Record Books of God are keeping now for men of this new age.

These stories of The Christ will be enough, for they contain the true philosophy of life, of death and of the resurrection of the dead.

They show the spiral journey of the soul until the man of earth and God are one for evermore.'

There is a prophecy concerning Levi and his commission given by Elihu the instructor of prophets in Zoan, Egypt says:

'This age will comprehend but little of the works of Purity and Love; but not a word is lost, for in the Book of God's Remembrance a registry is made of every thought and word and deed;

And when the world is ready to receive, lo, God will send a messenger to open up the book and copy from its sacred pages all the messages of Purity and Love.

Then every man of earth will read the words of life in the language of his native land, and men will see the light.

And man again will be at one with God.' - *AG* 7

III. Deity

God was at one time unmanifested, but chose to manifest. Through these manifestations of Deity the Universe was created. God created all living beings and manifests within all beings, in order to express His Love and to interact with those He loves. All Manifestations of Deity and all of creation are manifestations of God, just in different realms or dimensions of existence. Everything is a direct expansion of God through His will, and is made up of eternal components of ether (Spirit), matter and energy. God the One is known as Tao, Brahm, The I AM, the Word. This Universal Spirit may be called the Holy Spirit in a general sense. The Sacred Name, The Omnific Word encompasses the Universal Spirit or Breath. This is discussed further under The Omnific Word.

'Before the worlds were formed all things were One; just Spirit, Universal Breath. In early ages of the world the dwellers in the farther East said, Tao is the name of Universal Breath.'- *AG* 9

11

'In ancient times a people in the East were worshippers of God, the One, whom they called Brahm. In Persia Brahm was known...Men saw him as the One, the causeless Cause of all that is, and he was sacred unto them, as Tao to the dwellers of the farther East.'- *AG* 10

IV. The Triune God

The Triune God or Trinity is a direct manifestation through the breathing of God the One unmanifested. The Christine Triune God is the same as the Christian Trinity: God the Father is the Father God; God the Son is Christ; God the Holy Spirit is the Holy Breath or the Mother God. The Triune God may be considered abstractly as Power (Father), Wisdom (Mother) and Love (Christ the Son); and impersonally as Energy (Father), Matter (Mother) and Light (Christ the Son), or as Albert Einstein expressed this equation as $E=mc2$ (Energy = mass X the speed of light squared).

'And Spirit breathed, and that which was not became the Fire and the Thought of heaven, the Father-God, the Mother-God. And when the Fire and Thought of heaven in union breathed, their son, their only son, was born. This son is Love whom men have called the Christ. Men call the Thought of heaven the Holy Breath.' - *AG* 9: 16-18

'Eternal Thought is one; in essence it is two - Intelligence

13

and Force; and when they breathe a child is born; this child is Love.

And thus the Triune God stands forth, whom men call Father-Mother-Child.

This Triune god is one; but like the one of light, in essence he is seven.'- *AG* 58: 19-21

'Before creation was the Christ walked with the Father God and Mother God in Akasha. The Christ is son, the only son begotten by Almighty God, the God of Force and God omniscient, God of thought; and Christ is God, the God of Love.'- *AG, The Christ*

The Father God is the Will, the Force, the Power and the Fire of heaven and earth - the universe. He is called by different names around the world and the names mentioned in The AG are: the Father-God,

Parabrahm, Thoth, Zeus and Jehovah. Much speculation over the centuries allows for differences in the assignments of each of these names to particular parts or attributes of Deity. Thoth was the Egyptian God who weighed the souls of the dead upon scales and was considered by many to be the Creator. The name Zeus, the King of the gods was used by the Greek philosophers as the name for God. Jehovah is used sometimes to mean all aspects of God the One and the Triune God and is actually the corrupted substitute for the True Name of God JAHHEVAHE, but in Christine usage Jehovah refers to the Father God. This will be discussed in greater detail under the chapter entitled *The Omnific Word.*

'... Every nation sees a part of God, and every nation has a name for God. You Brahamans call him Parabrahm; in Egypt he is Thoth; and Zeus is his name in Greece; Jehovah is his Hebrew name; but everywhere he is the causeless Cause, the rootless Root from which all things have grown.'- *AG* 28

Spirit Consciousness or Consciousness of the Omnipotence of God and man is the understanding that all things are possible with God, that we can and must become one with God. Through this knowledge we learn that God is the Force that is the Source of all our Power that beats our heart and gives us life and every good thing for our use.

'The twelve apostles now had reached the stage of spirit consciousness, and Jesus could reveal to them the deeper meanings of his mission to the world.'- *AG* 124: 1

The Mother God is the Thought and Wisdom of heaven and earth - the Universe. She is called by different names in the *AG* such as Visel, the Goddess Wisdom, the Holy Breath and the Comforter. Visel means 'life energy'(vis) of 'God'(el) or God Energy. 'Vis' also conveys the meanings of "expanse," "vision," and "wisdom." It is related to the words 'wise' and 'wit' in English; and in Sanskrit, a cognate for 'vidya'("wisdom") and 'veda'("knowledge"; "scripture"). When the Father-God and Mother-God breathed in unison Christ the Son was born. Thus, the Mother-God may be referred to as the 'Immaculate Concept' (idea) and 'Immaculate Conception' (impregnation and delivery) that produced Love, which is Christ. This belief in the femininity of Deity may seem new and foreign to many, but this Mighty Truth is an ancient belief and will be discussed further because of the need of greater clarity on this subject.

'And then the goddess Wisdom spoke, and with her hands outstretched she poured the benedictions of the Holy Breath upon the rulers of Aquarius.'- *AG, The Cusp of the Ages*

Visel, the Holy Breath (Spirit) is the Goddess Wisdom. She is the Comforter spoken of by Jesus.

She manifested as a Dove and alighted on Jesus' head in *AG* 55: 10 & 64: 12. Levi S. Dowling in his book *Self Culture* devotes a whole chapter, Lesson VII on the Holy Spirit. There are also many references to the Goddess Wisdom in scripture. There are numerous references to the Mother God, the Goddess Wisdom in *Proverbs*, where she is referred to as Wisdom. In Greek translations of the Bible and in Gnostic scriptures, Our Heavenly Mother is known as Sophia which means "wisdom." Here are some important passages:

The Words of Wisdom, the Mother God:

'Behold, I will pour out my spirit unto you, I will make known my words unto you.' - *Proverbs* 1: 23 *KJV*

'Happy is the man that findeth Wisdom, and the man that getteth understanding...Length of days is in her right hand; and in her left hand riches and honour. Her ways are ways of pleasantness, and all her paths are peace. She is a tree of life to them that lay hold upon her: and happy is every one that retaineth her. The LORD by Wisdom hath founded the earth; by understanding hath he established the heavens.' - *Proverbs* 3: 13-19 *KJV*

'Wisdom is the principal thing; therefore get Wisdom: and with all thy getting get understanding. Exalt her, and she shall promote thee: she shall bring thee to honour, when thou dost embrace her. She shall give to thine head an ornament of grace: a crown of glory shall she deliver to thee.' - *Proverbs* 4: 7-9 *KJV*

The Mother God is mentioned in the New Testament:
'Wisdom is justified of her children.' - *Matthew* 12: 19; *Luke* 8: 35, *KJV*
'The Wisdom that is from above is first pure, then peaceable, gentle, easy to be entreated, full of mercy and good fruits, without partiality and without hypocrisy.' - *James* 3: 17, *KJV*

Levi translates the Spirit of Truth as 'she' in the following passage in his book *SC*, Pg. 88:
'Howbeit when she, the Spirit of Truth is come, she will guide you into all truth.' - John 16: 13, *KJV*

The AG teaches that the Christ, the Son of the Mother God, was conceived without carnal knowledge, but a Spiritual and Perfect or Immaculate Conception. The Virgin Mother is the Mother God, the Goddess Wisdom. Many believe that Mary, the mother of Jesus, conceived and gave birth to the Christ Child, while yet a virgin. Many other Great Beings who embodied or manifested as prophets, founders of religions and Manifests of Christ are also said to be born of virgin mothers, such as: Gautama Buddha, Krishna and Zarathustra. The teaching of Jesus being born of a virgin piously held by Christians is not here to be refuted, but brought greater clarity. Officially, the Aquarian Christine Church, Inc. **does not teach the virgin birth doctrine, nor refute, deny or condemn it,** nor any belief such as this regarding the births of Buddha, Krishna or Zarathustra.

Holy Breath Consciousness is the Consciousness of Supreme Intelligence. This consciousness is obtained by sensitizing oneself to the finer vibrations of the primary substance of the universe called Akasha. By doing this, one taps into the Universal Mind which pervades and records all activities in the universe.

'Then Jesus left the wilderness and in the consciousness of Holy Breath, he came unto the camps of John and taught.'- *AG* 65: 17

Christ is **God the Son**, He is referred to as the Day Star, the Sun of Righteousness, Love, Life, Light and the Logos (which means 'word' in Greek). It is said Christ is the oil of life and Christ means anointed in Greek and means the same as the word Messiah or Mashich. He is called Krishna or Krisht in Hinduism; Krishna means 'all-attractive' or 'deep blue.' The words used at the Resurrection by the Silent Brotherhood of Masters (clothed in shimmering white), also known as the Great White Brotherhood, were 'Adon Mashich Cumi!' which means 'Lord Christ Arise!' In Aquarian Christine teaching Jesus the Christ is the head of the Great White Brotherhood.

Jesus was a man who conquered his lower or carnal nature and was able to manifest Christ, God the Son, within Him fully. Enoch and Melchisedec also manifested the Christ each in or around 2,000 year intervals, and there have been others. These three great manifestations of Christ will be discussed later. Throughout the Universe every Sun, Star and World has been sent a master spirit who manifests the Christ, Messiah or Anointed One. We also may manifest the Christ within us, perform miracles, Resurrect and Ascend; this belief is called **Christ Consciousness** or **Consciousness of Divine Love**.

'Without the Christ there was no light. Through Christ all life was manifest; and naught was done in forming worlds or peopling of worlds without the Christ. Christ is the Logos of Infinities and through the Word alone are Thought and Force made manifest. The Son is called the Christ, because the Son, the Love, the universal Love, was set apart, ordained to be creator, Lord, preserver and redeemer of all things, of everything that is, or evermore will be.

Now Christ, the universal Love, pervades all spaces of infinity, and so there is no end to love.

'To every world and star and moon and sun a master spirit of this Love divine was sent; and all were full anointed with the oil of helpfulness, and each become a Christ. All glorious in his majesty is Christ who spreads the pure white robe of Love o'er all the planes of earth - The Christ of earth, its heaven, its graves.' - *AG, The Christ*

The purpose in the establishment of the Aquarian Christine Church is to manifest and expand the Kingdom of God within the individual and the world. Each member is a priest or priestess and a king or queen. Each may be or become a prophet or prophetess and seer, this is someone who may expound the Will and Wisdom of God to others; they may dream dreams and have visions as well. When one has attained the trinity of consciousnesses - Spirit, Christ and Holy Breath Consciousnesses - they have risen to the plane of **Christine Consciousness**.

'And Jesus said, I cannot show the king unless you see with eyes of soul, because the kingdom of the king is in the soul. And every soul a kingdom is. There is a king for every man. This king is love, and when this love becomes the greatest power in life, it is the Christ; so Christ is king.

And every one may have this Christ dwell in his soul, as Christ dwells in my soul. The body is the temple of the king, and men may call a holy man a king.

A king of heaven may wear a fisher's garb; may sit in mart of trade; may till the soil, or be a gleaner in the field; may be a slave in mortal chains; may be adjudged a criminal by men; may languish in a prison cell; may die upon a cross. The man of God is pure in heart; he sees the king; he sees with eyes of soul; and when he rises to the plane of Christine consciousness, he knows that he himself is king, is love, is Christ, and so is son of God.' - *AG* 71

Christine consciousness may be explained as the one who makes a confession of faith in Christ, practices the teachings and progresses through the levels of consciousness, becomes not only a member of the Church, but becomes incorporated into the living body that is the Church. This is mystically and metaphysically explained through the symbolism of rebirth and marriage. The Mother-God or Holy Breath enters you, you enter Her, or return to Her, and are born again and become Her child. This child (the Church collectively and the Kingdom of Heaven) is her daughter Christine and is preparing to be married to the Bridegroom - Christ. The Bride of Christ (we Christines, the Church and the Kingdom of Heaven) is coming to her wedding feast and as a husband and wife become one body in marriage, we are becoming one with Christ and the Father. He enters us, we share in His Perfection and we become the Fourth Member of the Triune God or Trinity, forming a Quaternity, a grafted

Branch to the Vine, through adoption by or rather returning to the Father and Mother.

The ultimate goal is to master all these levels of consciousness and become fully Divine called a Master and Ascend or more specifically become an Ascended Master. This is achieved by raising the consciousness until nothing in the individual but Divinity remains, or all is transmuted into Divinity; in the material world, the Realm of Manifest, it is called the Resurrection of the body; in the Realms of Soul and Spirit it is called the Ascension.

V. The Omnific Word

The most sacred name of God is the Word, the Logos, the Omnific Word. The substitute Jehovah has been handed down to us in a corrupted form as an attempt to pronounce the Hebrew four letter word for the name of God, the Tetragram. The true pronunciation was lost for centuries. It fell into disuse in Judaism, because it was understood by the high priests and scribes, and understood correctly, that it is too sacred to be profaned in any way. Now today, The AG restores the proper Name and pronunciation of the Word, it is JAHHEVAHE. The Omnific Word is pronounced yah - hay - vah - hay. Surprisingly the meaning of the Name has always been preserved. Jahhevahe means 'I AM That I AM' or more precisely 'I AM That (Which) I AM'. The Word was revealed unto Moses by God in response to Moses asking God while manifested in a Flame of Fire in the Burning Bush what his people should call Him. The Omnific Word and the I AM represent the Universal Breath, the Universal Spirit (Brahm; Tao) that manifests within us all as our Divine Self, our I AM Spirit (Mighty I AM Presence; the Higher Self; one's angel; Guardian Angel).

'And Moses said unto God, Behold, when I come unto the children of Israel, and shall say unto them, The God of your fathers hath sent me unto you; and they shall say to me, What is his name? What shall I say unto them?

And God said unto Moses, I AM That I AM: and he said, Thus shalt thou say unto the children of Israel, I AM hath sent me unto you.' - *Exodus* 3: 13-14, *KJV*

'The Logos is the perfect word; that which creates; that which destroys and that which saves.' - *AG* 48: 3

Jesus uses the Omnific Word to heal a blind man:
'Then Jesus called the man and said, Would you be free? Would you receive your sight?

The man replied, All that I have would I most freely give if I could see.

And Jesus took saliva and a bit of clay and made a salve, and put it on the blind man's eyes.

He spoke the Word and then he said, Go to Siloam and wash, and as you wash say, Jahhevahe. This do for seven times and you shall see.

The man was led unto Siloam; he washed his eyes and spoke the word, and instantly his eyes were opened and he saw.' - *AG* 138: 18-22

The I AM is used throughout The *AG* by Jesus when

making important metaphysical statements, such as I AM the Resurrection and the Life, a very powerful statement that all may decree. Use of the Jahhevahe, the "I AM" and "I AM That I AM" produce a particular vibration as they are spoken that invoke Divinity, one's own Divinity, in a profound and dynamic way.

The Aquarian Christine Church believes it is the only religion in possession of the True Name of God, the Word, the Logos. The Church also believes it is <u>too sacred to be profaned in any way</u>, used in normal everyday and <u>common speech and conversations</u>, <u>spoken in front of unbelievers</u> and/or <u>irreverent persons</u>, used in any other way other than invoking God, healing, blessing, prayer, meditation, etc.. Thus, the Aquarian Christines proclaim to each believer that We are the Keepers and Guardians of the Omnific Word! This is a privilege not to be taken lightly. All heaven and earth, spirits of fire, air, water and earth and disembodied souls and demonic spirits are compelled to obey at our command through the Power that is God. Floods, fires, tornadoes, earthquakes, sickness and even death may be averted by the use of the Sacred Name, the Omnific Word for the blessing of the world.

Scriptural References to the Divinity of and within Mankind:

'And Jesus said, A prophet of your own said to the sons of men, Lo, **you are gods**!' - *AG* 147: 19

'I have said, Ye are gods; and all of you are children of the most High.' - *Psalm* 82: 6 *KJV*

'Jesus answered them, Is it not written in your law, I said, Ye are gods?' - *John* 10:34 *KJV*

'And we have known and believed the love that God hath to us. **God is love; and he that dwelleth in love dwelleth in God, and God in him.**' - 1 *John* 4: 16 *KJV*

Immersion in the Light and the Baptism in Fire:
One should imagine one immersed in a Pillar of bright white Light vibrating an almost electric blue about ten feet around you in every direction. Then one should imagine oneself Baptized in Violet Fire and Flame about three feet in every direction and above and below oneself. The color of the Violet Flame is a bright, electric bluish purple. This is the Immersion in the Light of God which purifies and the Baptism in Fire which transmutes all anger, negativity and karma. While visualizing this meditation, say the following decrees from *Aquarian Light* section of this book. An image or painting of this visualization is called a Veronica.

VI. The Elohim

Expanding from the Triune God or Trinity and incorporated into Deity, the Godhead, are Seven Divine Spirits
who are the creative and sustaining Spirits of the Universe.
These Seven Spirits are also known as the Septonate and
the Lesser Gods in the AG. They are masculine and feminine and we were created in Their Image-male and female.

'And when the Triune God breathed forth, lo, seven
Spirits stood before the throne. These are the Elohim,
creative spirits of the universe.

And these are they who said, Let us make man; and in
their image man was made.' - *AG* 9: 19-20

'This Triune God is one; but like the one of light, in
essence he is seven.

And when the Triune God breathes forth, lo, seven
Spirits stand before his face; these are creative attributes.

Men call them lesser gods, and in their image they
made man.' - *AG* 58: 21-23

In *Revelation,* The Elohim are the Seven Spirits:

'Grace be unto you, and peace, from him which is, and which was, and which is to come; and from **the seven Spirits which are before his throne.'** - *Revelation* 1: 4 *KJV*

'And I beheld, and, lo, in the midst of the throne...and in the midst of the elders, stood...**the seven Spirits of God sent forth into all the earth.'** - *Revelation* 5: 6 *KJV*

The Elohim are known as "the morning stars" in *Job:*
'Then the LORD answered Job out of the whirlwind, and said...Where wast thou when I laid the foundations of the earth?...When **the morning stars sang together, and all the sons of God shouted for joy?'** - *Job* 38 *KJV*

The Elohim have focuses in stars and constellations and this is reflected in their names. Some of the Elohim are mentioned by name in the Bible:

Which alone spreadeth out the heavens, and...which maketh **Arcturus, Orion,** and **Pleiades**, and the chambers of the south.' - *Job* 9: 8-9 *KJV*

'Canst thou bind the sweet influences of **Pleiades**, or loose the bands of **Orion**?' - *Job* 38: 31 *KJV*

'Seek him that maketh **the seven stars and Orion** ...' - *Amos* 5: 8 *KJV*

Not too long ago, competent translators of the original Hebrew, Aramaic and Greek sources used to compile the

Holy Bible who compiled the *NEB*, rediscovered other names of stars in *Job*, and are in the *NEB*. They are the Vintager or Vindemiatrix, the Grape Harvestress, a star in Virgo; Capella, a star near the constellation Perseus, which is near and has always been associated with Cassiopeia; and the Dog Star, Sirius, referred to esoterically as the "God Star."

The Elohim Arcturus - The Elohim Arcturus is the greatest of the Spirits who are before the Throne. The Elohim Arcturus is mirror-like in that reflects all of the other Elohim within himself. The Elohim Arcturus has a focus in the star Arcturus within the constellation Bootes.

The Aspect of Arcturus for our solar system and the earth is known as Sanat Kumara or Ahura Mazda. In other religious traditions He is known as: **Ahura Mazda** in Zoroastrianism; **Sanat Kumara** in Hinduism; and as the Adi-Buddha and Brahma Sanam Kumara in Buddhism. Ahura Mazda is also referred to as the **Ancient of Days** in *Daniel*.

'... canst thou guide **Arcturus with his sons**?' - *Job* 38: 32 *KJV*

'The greatest of the Spirits standing near the throne is the Ahura Mazda, who manifests in brightness of the sun.

And all the people saw Ahura Mazda in the sun, and they fell down and worshipped him in temples of the sun.' - *AG* 10: 24-25

The Elohim Arcturus bestows the gift of the Violet

Ray and the Violet Flame, which transmutes karma and negativity and is the most important of all the Sacred Fires.

The Elohim of Peace - The Elohim of Peace bestows the gift of the Purple and Gold Ray of Mercy, Peace and Tranquility and the Purple Flame of Grace and Mercy.

Jesus the Christ and Melchisedec were Hierarchs of the Purple and Gold Ray, thus both are known as the Prince of Peace. The Elohim of Peace is thought of as the **Goddess of Peace**. Like the Mother Goddess, the Elohim of Peace is represented by the Dove, and is referred to as the Dove of Peace in *AG* 76: 9.

The Aspect of Peace for our solar system and the earth is the **Goddess of Dawn**, referred to as the **Dawn of Peace** in *AG* 113: 2, and was known anciently as Eos in the Greek Religion (Aurora in the Roman); Ushah in Zoroastrianism; and Ushas in Hinduism. The Dawn is associated with the atmosphere, which serves as a vessel for the Holy Breath of Life, the Mother God. According to "Encyclopedic Theosophical Glossary," 'Mystically, the dawn is the bringer of spiritual and intellectual light, and therefore the sweet and Holy Comforter, allusions to which are found even in the *New Testament* with reference to the Paraclete.' [1]

The Elohim Cyclopea - The Elohim Cyclopea is the **All Seeing Eye** of God and has a focus in the constellation of the Pleiades. The Pleiades are mentioned in *Job*. Cyclopea means "circle-eyed" and represents singleness of vision. In the year 2000, the constellation of the Pleiades left its home in Taurus and moved into Gemini and on an seemingly inevitable path toward Cancer. This is considered in esoteric circles as not only being a sign and wonder, but the inauguration of the entrance into the Age of Aquarius.

The Elohim Cyclopea is connected with singleness of Spiritual Vision and the Third Eye above and between the brows. The regular depiction of the All-Seeing Eye or the Egyptian Eye of Horus is the proper visualization. Cyclopea is referred to as "the Eyes of Holy Breath" in the *AG*.

The All Seeing Eye is associated with Divine Providence and the myriad of modern scientific advances, discoveries and inventions. Cyclopea is the Elohim of the Emerald Green and Aqua Ray of Healing, Music, Science and Supply. Cyclopea bestows the Emerald Green and Aqua Flame of Healing and Supply. It is said the **Great Silent Watcher** is the Aspect of Cyclopea for the planet Earth. Every person's Divine I AM Spirit is the Silent Watcher and All-Seeing Eye for their own life stream.

The Elohim of Purity - The Elohim of Purity is the **Goddess of Purity,** and is associated with the star called Vindemiatrix in Virgo. Vindemiatrix or the Vintager is mentioned in *Job* in the *NEB*. The Aspect of the Elohim of Purity for our solar system and the earth is **Astrea** (Astraea), known anciently as the Goddess of Justice that left her association with the earth and mankind when they became corrupt and retreated to the constellation Virgo, was crowned with the constellation Coma Berenices and holds aloft the Balances of Libra. She is referred to as **Purity** in the *AG*. John the Harbinger (Baptist) was the Manifest of Purity.

Mighty Astrea is said to wield the Sword of Blue Flame and bestows the White Flame of Hope and Purtiy. Astrea also bestows the Fiery Christ Blue Lightning which destroys discord, evil, karma and negativity. It oscillates a bright Blue and White fire and flame. [2] Mighty Astrea also bestows the gift of the White Ray of Hope, Purity and Resurrection.

The Elohim Orion - The Elohim Orion has a focus in the constellation Orion and is the Elohim of Love. Orion means "the Light of Heaven." He is referred to as **"Love Divine"** in the *AG*; and was known anciently as **Eros** in the Greek Religion. Eros, as the concept of Love, was considered in Greek Religion as a Great and Mighty Cosmic Being behind the creation and workings of the Universe. The Elohim Orion bestows the gift of the soft, light Pink Ray and Flame of Love, associated with the Love that is Christ. The Aspect of the Elohim Orion for our solar system and earth is **Sananda** Kumara. He is associated with Life and Love which one promotes and produces the other; i.e. Life produces Love (filial, familial, romantic and adoptive) which in turn produces and promotes Life. Jesus the Christ was the Manifest of Love, the Love that is Christ and Sananda, the Elohim of Love.

The Elohim Cassiopeia - The Elohim Cassiopeia has a focus in the constellation Cassiopeia. He was known anciently as **Apollo** in Greek and Roman Religion; Horus and Ra in Egyptian Religion; Mitra in Hinduism; and Mithras in the Mithraic Mysteries. He is still known today in Zoroastrianism as Mithra, and is associated with the constellation Perseus, which neighbors Cassiopeia and have always been associated with each other in myth and legend.

The Solar Ruler of our sun is **Helios** (Heloi in the *AG,*) an Aspect of Cassiopeia. The Elohim Cassiopeia bestows the gift of the Yellow Ray of Wisdom and the Golden Flame of Illumination.

The Elohim Hercules - The Elohim Hercules has a focus in constellation Hercules. Our sun is speeding through space on a path directly towards a point within the constellation Hercules. An Aspect of Hercules is **Surya**, who is associated with the star Sirius, who is mentioned in *Job* in the *NEB*. Surya is known as the **Elohim of Sirius** and his Cherubic Aspect is known as the Maitreya, who embodied as Krishna. It is taught by the Ascended Masters that Surya and the Maitreya are really one and the same.

[3] Surya means 'God's Command' in Hebrew and should not necessarily be identified with Surya, the Vedic sun god. Surya is the Aspect of Hercules for the earth and our solar system.

The name Hercules in Greek is Heracles ('the glory of the air') and is related to Hare Krisht (Hare Krishna). Hare Krishna means the Strength of Christ.

Hercules is referred to as **Strength** in the *AG* and he embodies and bestows this virtue. The Elohim Hercules wields the Sword of Blue Flame, and bestows the Blue Flame and Fiery Christ Blue Lightning of Protection, which destroys discord, evil, karma and negativity. Hercules bestows the gift of the Blue Ray of Power and Protection.

Sacred Colors - The sacred colors of the Christine Church are the colors used in the Temple of Heliopolis, the Great Lodge of the Heavens and Earth and are directly associated with the Rays and Flames bestowed by the Seven Mighty Elohim. They are Blue, Yellow, soft light Pink, Lavender, White, Aqua, Emerald Green, Gold, Purple, and Violet. Robes and church furnishings reflect this belief, they are sacred and of holy vibration. They are the colors of Royalty, the Heavenly Sky, many flowers and birds, and of Pure Fire and Flame. Basically the colors that are not sacred are Black, Brown, Grey, Red, Scarlet, Crimson, hot Pink, Peach, Orange and murky and yellowish (jaundice-like, sickish) shades of Green.

'All glorious in his majesty is Christ who spreads the

pure **white** robe of Love o'er all the planes of earth.' - *AG, The Christ*

'**White** is the symbol of the virtuous and pure!' - *AG* 76: 9

'The Logos waited seven days, and then was taken to the Hall of Fame, a chamber rich in furnishings, and lighted up with **gold** and **silver** lamps. The colors of its ceilings, decorations, furnishings and walls were **blue** and **gold**.' - *AG* 50: 1-2

'The work of Jesus...was done, and in the temple **purple** room he stood before the hierophant, And he was clothed in **purple** robes ...' - *AG* 55: 1-2

Levi further explains the symbolism and meaning of color in *SC* and refers to this teaching about color as "the mystic color scale:"

'**Yellow** embraces the characteristics of Intelligence.' - *SC*, Pg. 34 *paraphrased*

'**Green** is the color of growth and is the symbol of Immortality...**Purple** is Royalty, Exaltation, Honor ...' - *SC*, Pg. 35

'... motherly Love...is a **delicate Pink**.' - SC, Pg. 37

VII. The Fall, Three Realms and Seven Planes

There are three realms of existence for everything in the Universe: the Realm of Spirit, the Realm of Soul and the Realm of Manifest. The Realm of Spirit is the original perfect and divine realm; the Kingdom of Heaven pervades this realm and expands (is expanding) into the other realms. The Realm of Soul is a lower vibratory and thicker realm than the Realm of Spirit. Within this realm is the Kingdom of the Soul, known as Paradise or Eden, an expansion of the Kingdom of Heaven into this realm of soul. Souls of the departed that are not pure enough to enter the Kingdom through sin and karma are purified in the Purifying Fires or Purgatory. The Realm of Manifest is our current realm of physical existence; it is lowest vibratory and densest realm. It is basically Hell, but the Kingdom of Heaven (a state of mind, consciousness and grace) has now come and is expanding into this realm. It is the only realm where evil exists. Souls unable to or who do not desire to rise unto the Realm of Soul and to the Purifying Fires, are ghosts and haunt the atmosphere of this lower Realm of Manifest in a state of Limbo.

There are **Seven Planes of Created Beings** created by the Seven Mighty Elohim at the direction of the Triune God. The Seven Planes are: the Cherubim (and Seraphim); the Angels; Mankind; Animals; Plants; Protoplast, meaning microscopic life and cellular structures; and Earth, meaning the elements and the elemental spirits of fire, air, water and earth. The Cherubim (and Seraphim), the Angels and Man are the truly sentient, aware and conscious beings who are the most perfect reflections of Deity and are created in Their Image. The Cherubim (and Seraphim) and Angels did not fall; all the rest fell into the Realm of Manifest.

'Time never was when man was not...man himself is not the body, nor the soul; he is a spirit and is part of God. Creative Fiat gave to man, to spirit man, a soul that he might function on the plane of soul; gave him a body of the flesh, that he might function on the plane of things made manifest.'

'Man is a thought of God; all thoughts of God are infinite; they are not measured up by time ... The thoughts of God are from the everlasting ... unto the never ending days to come – And so is man, the Spirit-Man.'

'Without a foe a soldier never knows his strength, and thought must be developed by the exercise of strength. And so this carnal nature soon became a foe that man must fight, that he might be the strength of God made manifest ... Man is the Lord of all the plane of manifests; of protoplast, of mineral, of plant, of beast; but he has given up his birthright, just to gratify his lower self, his carnal self.

But man will full regain his lost estate, his heritage; but he must do it in a conflict ... he must suffer trials and temptations manifold ... Man will be fully saved, redeemed, perfected by the things he suffers on the plane of flesh, and on the plane of soul.'

'Man cannot die; the spirit man is one with God ... when man has conquered every foe upon the plane of soul ... man will then attain unto the blessedness of perfectness and be at one with God.' - *AG, Man*

Levi speaks of the Soul in his book *SC*:
'The Soul is a body like the physical; or perhaps it would be better to say that the physical is built according to the pattern of the soul. The soul senses correspond exactly with the physical; the soul sees, hears, smells, tastes, feels and telepaths.' - *SC*, Pg. 61
'... all forms of life on every plane are thoughts of God, all creatures think, and every creature is possessed of will, and, in its measure, has the power to choose,

And in their native planes all creatures are supplied with nourishment from the ethers of their planes.

And so it was with every living thing until the will

became a sluggish will ... and then the ethers of the proto-plast, the earth, the plant, the beast, the man ... all became more dense, and ... were clothed with coarser garbs, the garbs of flesh ... and thus this coarser manifest, which men call physical, appeared.

And this is what is called **the fall of man; but man fell not alone, for protoplast, and earth, and plant and beast were all included in the fall.**

The angels and the cherubim fell not; their wills were ever strong, and so they held the ethers of their planes in harmony with God.

Now, when the ethers reached the rate of atmosphere (and all the creatures of these planes must get their food from atmosphere) the conflict came; and then that which the finite man has called survival of the best, became a law.

The stronger ate the bodies of the weaker manifests; and here is where the carnal law of evolution had its rise.

In yonder kingdom of the soul this carnal evolution is not known, and the great work of master minds is to re-store the heritage of man, to bring him back to his estate that he has lost, when he again will live upon the ethers of his native plane.

The thoughts of God change not; the manifests of life on every plane unfold into perfection of their kind; and as the thoughts of God can never die, **there is no death to any being of the seven ethers** of the seven Spirits of the Triune God.' - *AG* 32

Levi in his book *Biopneuma*, further explains The Fall as part and parcel of the **Great Disaster**:

'... until the "Great Disaster," which has ever marked the period called the "Fall of Man," men maintained perfect health, and Love was pure, Intelligence perfect, and Will divine. The Genesis historian (Chapter 6) describes the men of those primeval times as "Sons of God," and 'giants" and long-lived.

The Great Disaster - There was a time when a terrible disaster befell the earth . The word disaster means "an astral calamity, a trouble caused by the stars," and the Great Disaster, to which reference here made, was so terrible that it shook the earth to its very center, tipped it twenty-three and one-half degrees from its original position, and disarranged the order of all terrestrial things. A great planet whose benign influence had been the energizing, vitalizing force of the respiratory organs of men, was totally destroyed, and the great Breath ceased to find an abiding-place in the human body. But **the physical Disaster was only a reflex of a great moral disaster, for which the will of men was responsible**, - a calamity that inaugurated the despotism of Evil and alienated the human race from the heart of the Everlasting Father. As a result, the way to the Tree of life was obstructed. In that wonderful symbolic representation fo the fall of man, and his exclusion from the glorious Eden, recorded in Genesis ...' - *Biopneuma*, Pp. 6-7

Heaven is not far away:

'Lo, you have solved a mystery; **you are within the kingdom and the kingdom is in you.**' - *AG* 155: 31

'And Jesus said, My brother, man, your thoughts are wrong; your **heaven is not far away**; and it is not a place of metes and bounds, is not a country to be reached; **it is a state of mind.**

God never made a heaven for man; he never made a hell; we are creators and we make our own.

Now, cease to seek for heaven in the sky; just **open up the windows of your hearts, and, like a flood of light, a heaven will come and bring a boundless joy**; then toil will be no cruel task.' - *AG* 33: 8-10

Life is Eternal:

'And Jesus said ... in the world to come, and in the resurrection day, men do not take upon themselves the marriage vows.

But, **like the angels and the other sons of God**, they form not unions for the pleasure of the self, nor to perpetuate the race.

Death does not mean the end of life. The grave is not the goal of men, no more than is the earth the goal of seeds.

Life is the consequence of death. The seed may seem to die, but from its grave the tree arises into life.

So man may seem to die, but he lives on, and **from the grave he springs up into life.**

If you could comprehend the word that Moses spoke about the burning bush that burned and still was not consumed, then you would know that death cannot destroy the life.' - *AG* 155: 14-19

The Purifying Fires, or Purgatory:

'And Jesus said, God's kingdom is a duality; it has an outer and an inner form.

As seen by man it is composed of men, of those who make confession of the name of Christ.

The inner kingdom is the kingdom of the soul, the kingdom of the pure in heart.

Hear, then, the meaning of the parable of the wheat and tares:

The sower is the son of man; the field, the world; the good seed are the children of the light; the tares, the children of the dark; the enemy, the carnal self; the harvest day, the closing of the age; the reapers are the messengers of God.

The reckoning day will come to every man; then will the tares be gathered up, and cast into the fire and be burned.

Then will **the good shine forth as suns in the kingdom of the soul.**

And Philip said, Must men and women suffer in the flames because they have not found the way of life?

And Jesus said, **The fire purifies.** The chemist throws into the fire the ores that hold all kinds of dross.

The useless metal seems to be consumed; but **not a grain of gold is lost.**

There is no man that has not in him gold that cannot be destroyed. The evil things of men are all consumed in fire; the gold survives.' - *AG* 116

Ghosts in Limbo:
'Now, spirits of the lately dead that cannot rise to higher planes, remain about the tombs that hold the flesh and bones of what was once their mortal homes.

They sometimes take possession of the living, whom they torture in a hundred ways.' - *AG*: 118: 5-6

Souls who have risen to the Realm of Soul, and the Spirts of the Resurrected and the Spirits of the Ascended Masters <u>are not ghosts</u>:
'If you believe that I AM phantom made of air, come forth and handle me; ghosts do not carry flesh and bones.

I came to earth to demonstrate **the resurrection of the dead, the transmutation of the flesh of carnal man to flesh of man divine.'** - *AG* 177: 18-19

God has given us power over the elemental spirits; as demonstrated by Jesus the Christ when he calmed the waters and the storm:
'And Jesus stood; he raised his hand; he talked unto the spirits of the winds and waves as men would talk with men.

And, lo, the winds blew not; the waves came

tremblingly and kissed his feet; the sea was calm.

And then he said, You men of faith, where is your faith? for you can speak and winds and waves will hear and will obey.' - *AG* 117

We have power over elemental spirits and can command legions of angels, but we should try to do things on our own and reserve this power only for times of emergency. We should be righteous in our ways and only command elemental spirits in purity of faith. And, we should be trained in how to practice the art of magic properly.

'But we are masters of the things of time. Lo, we can speak, and all the spirits of the fire, water, earth and air will stand in our defense.

We can command and many legions of the angel world would come and strike our enemies to earth.

But it is best that not a power of heaven or earth should come to our relief. And it is best that even God should veil his face and seem to hear us not.

As I AM pattern unto you, so you are patterns for the human race. We show by non-resistance that we give our lives in willing sacrifice for man.' - *AG* 127

'Now, **you can demonstrate the power of God**. Have faith in God, and you can bid the mountains to depart, and they will crumble at your feet; and **you may talk to wind and wave, and they will hear, and will obey what you command.**

God hears the prayer of faith and when you ask in faith you shall receive.

You may not ask amiss; God will not hear the prayer of any man who comes to him with blood of other men upon his hands.

And he who harbors envious thoughts, and does not love his fellow men, may pray forever unto God, and he will hear him not.

God can do nothing more for men than they would do for other men.' - *AG* 153: 6-11

'The art of magic is the art of employing invisible or so-called spiritual agencies to obtain certain visible results. God, the supreme magician, makes all things according to the eternal law of magic.' - *SC*, Pg. 74

VIII. The Cherubim and Seraphim, The Four and Twenty Elders

The Cherubim and Seraphim encircle the throne of God. They are known as "the four and twenty elders" and the "demi-gods" in the *AG*. They often are referred to and given the title of Cosmic Being. The cherubim are male and the seraphim are female and in pairs each rule a constellation or house of the zodiac. At the turn of each age, the rulership of the age is passed from one pair of cherubim and seraphim to the next. In the section of *The AG* called *The Cusp of the Ages*, Levi witnesses the transition from the Piscean to the Aquarian Age. The Piscean rulers were the cherubim Rama (Ramasa) and the seraphim Vacabiel. They passed their crown and scepter to the cherubim Archer (Aquaria) and the seraphim Akmaquil (s'Akmaquil). These names correspond with the nomenclature of Eliphas Levi and contain many prefixes, syllables and suffixes using "s" and "sa" meaning 'one who' or 'one that' as a title and to keep the uninitiated from learning their true names. [4]   The better known names of the cherubim and seraphim are found in *The Law of Life and Teachings of Divine Beings, Book I* by A.D.K. Luk. [5]

The Christine teaching is that the twelve cherubim and twelve seraphim are the four and twenty elders in *Revelation.*

This system called Astrochristology is now aligned exactly with the months and is more scientifically accurate than astrology, which is considered superstition and negative as is all fortune telling, horoscopes, channeling spirits, mediums, and black magic. This system will also be accurate for the next 720 years when it will again be affected by precession and will move forward another ten days each month. The Aquarian Christine Church teaches that the Christian calendar as it is now, is the most perfect and accurate of all calendars, including the days starting at midnight, as do all the major Holy Days traditionally. One need only fourteen calendars perpetually because the exact order of days repeats in cycles. This cycle of fourteen years represents the perfection of the calendar and the perfection of the Creative Spirits, the Seven Mighty Elohim and their aspects.

'In Spirit I was caught away into the realms of Akasha; I stood alone within the circle of the sun.

I saw the four and twenty Cherubim and Seraphim that guard the circle of the sun, the mighty ones who were proclaimed by masters long ago "the four and twenty ancient ones."

I heard the names of every Cherubim and Seraphim, and learned that every sign in all the Zodiac is ruled by two - a Cherubim and Seraphim.

And then I stood upon the cusp where ages meet. The Piscean Age had passed; the Aquarian Age had just begun.'- *AG, The Cusp of the Ages*

When the sun is in one of the constellations of the zodiac: the earth, the sun and the constellation are in alignment. Each month the corresponding Cherubim and Seraphim (Aspects of the Elohim) pour out their blessings on the Earth and bestow the gifts of each of their particular virtues when they are invoked. These twelve virtues are referred to as the "Twelve Immortal Thoughts" in *AG* 60: 10.

'But man will full regain his lost estate, his heritage; but he must do it in a conflict that cannot be told in words.

Yea, he must suffer trials and temptations manifold; but let him know that cherubim and seraphim that rule the stations of the sun, and spirits of the mighty God who rule the solar stars are his protectors and his guides, and they will lead to victory.' - *AG, Man*

Sagittarius - January - Virtue through invocation: *Enthusiasm*
Cherubim: Vuhori - "ruler of fire." He manifested as Enoch

the Christ and as the prophet and master Zarathustra; the Ruler of Sagittarius, the Ruler of the spirits of fire. [6] Zarathustra is also regarded as being a Manifest of Christ. He is known as **Prince Oromasis** memorializing him as the representative and aspect of Ahura Mazda or Oromasdes (Ormazd). He is often referred to as the **Prince of Fire** and **the Cosmic Zarathustra.**

Seraphim: Saritiel.

Invocation:
O Prince Oromasis, the Cosmic Zarathustra,
The Christ who stood upon the sun,
Thou Ruler of the spirits of fire,
Bestow upon us enthusiasm, each and every one.

Capricorn - February - Virtues through invocation: *Perception and Intuition*

Cherubim: s'Agdalon.

Seraphim: s'Emaquil - "wise fire"; "wise sky." **Minerva**, the Ruler of Capricorn is known also as **Athena**, who anciently was considered the goddess of wisdom. Like the Maha Chohan, she is an aspect of the Elohim Cassiopeia and the representative of the Goddess Wisdom, the Holy Breath, the Mother God.
Invocation:

O Mighty Cosmic Being Minerva,
Who leads us through each initiation,
Help us to perceive the ways of Our Mother,
And develop our spiritual intuition.
Aquarius - March - Virtues through invocation: *Progress & Spiritual Growth*

Cherubim: Archer, the Co-Ruler of the Aquarian Age.

Seraphim: s'Akmaquil - "bright mother of Aquila"; "spirit mother of Aquila; wise spirit mother." Known as **Quan Yin**; the Ruler of the Aquarian Age. Aquaria is also a name applied to Quan Yin, which is a name of the Mother God, as well. Quan Yin represents Divine Mercy and is known as the **Goddess of Mercy** in Taoism and Buddhism. She is of the Violet Ray and associated with the Lavender Flame, a combination of the Pink Flame of Love and the Violet Flame of Transmutation. Quan Yin is a feminine aspect of Ahura Mazda, who in Buddhism is known as Avolokiteshvara. It is taught esoterically that she embodied as a princess who became a nun and then ascended, therefore she is sometimes referred to as the Ascended Lady Master Quan Yin. .

Invocation:
Mighty Ruler of the Aquarian Age in the sky,
O Beloved Cosmic Being **Quan Yin**,
Pour out thy virtue of mercy upon us from on high, Blaze

through us the Violet Flame transmuting karma and sin.

Pisces - April - Virtue through invocation: *Purity*

Cherubim: Rama'sa - "delightful one." He is known in Hinduism as Rama, an Aspect of Surya **the Maitreya**. He is also known as Neptune, the Ruler of the spirits of water the water element, the moon and tides. He was the past Ruler of the Piscean Age which is associated with the Christian dispensation, he influenced the Rite of Baptism by water and such concepts as regeneration through water and the idea of holy water. The Maitreya overshadowed Jesus during his ministry. He **was** also known as Poseidon in Roman Religion; Napat-Apam (Apam Napat) in Hinduism and Zoroastrianism.

Seraphim: Vacabiel.

Invocation:
O Lord Maitreya, the Cosmic Christ,
Whose glory far outshines the moon,
Ruler of water, purify our soul and heart,
Mighty Cosmic Being Neptune.

Aries - May - Virtue through invocation: *Wisdom*
The esoteric emblem of Aries is the Lamb associated with the virtue of innocence; the "Lamb of Innocence" in *AG 76: 9*.
Cherubim: sa'Taaran - "heavenly one."

Seraphim: **s'**Arahiel - "sky altar"; "queen of God." Known as the Cosmic Being **Aries**, Ruler of the spirits of the air. Aries is the Seraphic Aspect of Aurora, the Dawn of Peace. She was the past Ruler of the Arian Age, the Age of the Judaic Dispensation; and, is also known in *AG* 19 as **Ariel**, the Patron Spirit of the city of Jerusalem and represents New Jerusalem, the Heavenly City. In invocation she should be addressed as the Cosmic Being Aries.

Invocation:
O Mighty Cosmic Being Aries,
Who rules the spirits of air and wind,
 Pour out upon us the virtue of wisdom,
Allowing our thoughts to ascend.

Taurus (Ox) - June - Virtues through invocation: *Faith, Strength, Courage and Power*

Cherubim: Bagdal - "valley of God." An Aspect of the Elohim Hercules, the Ruler of Taurus. In invocation he should be invoked as the Cosmic Being Hercules.
Seraphim: Araziel - "God is bright"; "God is truth."

Invocation:
O Mighty Cosmic Being Hercules,
Thou Cherubim of Blue Fiery Power,
Instill in us the virtue of Faith,
Increasing it each hour.

Gemini (Eden) - July - Virtues through invocation: *Love and Selflessness*

The esoteric emblem of Gemini is Adam and Eve on either side of the Tree of Knowledge, or the Tree of Life. Gemini, when depicted as the Twins, also represents the Buddha and Melchisedec the Christ (Krishna), who are both Aspects of the Maitreya. The Maitreya is the Cosmic Christ.

Cherubim: s'Agras - "leader." One Aspect manifested as Gautama Buddha and one Aspect manifested as Melchisedec the Christ and Krishna and is known as **the Maitreya**. The Maitreya is an Aspect of Surya, the Elohim of Sirius, who is also an Aspect of the Elohim Hercules (Hare Krishna.) All of whom are considered to have been a Manifest of Christ. Maitreya means the Lord of Love. In invocation he should be addressed as the Maitreya or Lord Maitreya.

Seraphim: Saraiel - "princess of God."

Invocation:
O Lord Maitreya, Thou Cosmic Christ,
The Prince of Peace and Lord of Love,
Instill in us thy virtue of selflessness,
From the Heavenly Kingdom above.

Cancer (Unicorn) - August - Virtues through invocation: *Concentration and Consecration*

Cherubim: Rahdar - "radar." An Aspect of the Elohim Cyclopea, the All Seeing Eye. In invocation he should be addressed as the Cosmic Being Cyclopea.
The All Seeing Eye is associated with Divine Providence, healing and scientific advances.

Seraphim: Phaquil - "wise light."

Invocation:
O Mighty Cosmic Being Cyclopea,
With thy Eye All Seeing,
develop in us greater concentration,
and consecrate our very Being.

Leo (Lion) - **September** - Virtues through invocation: *Courtesy and Dignity*

Cherubim: s'Agham - "the dawn." An Aspect of Helios the Solar Ruler who manifested as **Apollo,** one of the Seven Sages in the *AG*. He is known as the Ascended Master **the Maha Chohan.** He is an Aspect of the Elohim Cassiopeia and the Representative of the Holy Spirit, the Mother God; as is Minerva (Athena.)
'According to the "*Pistis Sophia*." the power of Sophia resides specially in the Solar Logos...' - *Encyclopedic Theosophical Glossary* [7]

Seraphim: Seratiel - "angel of God's light."

Invocation:
O Lord Maha Chohan of Divine Truth,
Thou Spirit Most Sanctified,
Pour out upon us thy courteous virtue,
Making our manners and actions dignified.

Virgo (Maiden) - October - Virtues through invocation:
Assurance and Confidence

Cherubim: Jadara (Iadara) - "one who holds water"; "gift of the light ray."

Seraphim: Schaltiel - "grain or Light of God's Peace." Known as **Virgo**; the Ruler of the spirits of the earth and the earth element. In this role she may be thought of as Mother Earth. She is the feminine Aspect of the Planetary Silent Watcher. Virgo was known anciently as Persephone in Greece and Proserpine in Rome, the daughter of Ceres (see Libra below.) In invocation she should be addressed as the Cosmic Being Virgo.

Invocation:
O Mighty Cosmic Being Virgo,
Thou Ruler of every earth spirit,
Upon us thy virtue of confidence bestow,
With assurance of Paradise mankind doth inherit.

Libra (Liberty) - November - Virtue through invocation: *Liberty*

The emblem of Libra is the Goddess of Liberty bearing aloft the torch of Illumination. The Cherubim and Seraphim of Libra are Aspects of Astrea, the Elohim of Purity

Cherubim: Grasgarben - "mighty sword-bearing son." He manifested as Manetho, the historian and high priest of Serapis (Osiris) of the Temple of Heliopolis in Egypt and in the Ascended Master State as, **Matheno** in the *AG*. He is known as the Ascended Master **Serapis**. He was known anciently as the god of nature and was called Osiris in Egyptian Religion, Dionysus in the Greek Religion and Liber (Bacchus) in the Roman Religion. The title Serapis Bey means esoterically "the Seraphic Lord," this refers to him working closely with all the Seraphim.

Seraphim: Hadaquil - "freedom of God"; "wise liberty." Liberty, often referred to as the **Goddess of Liberty**, was known anciently as Ceres in Roman Religion, Demeter in Greek Religion, and Isis in Egyptian Religion. The virtue of Liberty is referenced several times in the *AG*. She may be thought of as Mother Nature, and in this capacity represents the Mother God, the Holy Breath. Mighty Liberty depicted with her torch held high symbolizes Illumination and echoes the mythic search by torchlight for Persephone (Virgo) and Osiris (Serapis).

Invocation:

O Mighty Cosmic Being Liberty,
Lighting our way with thy torch of Sacred Fire,
Lead us unto the Eternal Freedom,
And with lofty thoughts our minds inspire.

Scorpio (Eagle) - December - Virtue through invocation: *Victory*

The emblem of Scorpio is the Eagle, referred to as the Bird of Justice and Righteousness in *AG 62: 8-21.* The constellation Aquila which means the Eagle was associated in ancient esoteric tradition with Scorpio because Aquila rises first on the horizon.

Cherubim: Riehol - "able one." Known as **Mighty Victory,** the Ruler of Scorpio, he bestows the virtue of Victory, referenced in *AG Man;* 49: 2. Mighty Victory is the Cherubic Aspect of Sananda Kumara. In invocation he should be addressed as the Cosmic Being Mighty Victory.

Seraphim: Sessael.

Invocation:

O Mighty Cosmic Being Mighty Victory,
With thee we rest assured along our Way,
That the final Triumph of the Ascension is near,
And Heaven will be on earth one great and glorious day.

The *AG* contains several references to Heavenly bodies; for instance, Jesus being the Manifest of the Christ, is referred to as **"The Day Star from on High"** and as **"The Sun of Righteousness:"**

'Behold, for soon the Day Star from on high will visit us, to light the way for those who sit within the darkness of the shadow-land, and guide our feet unto the ways of peace. - *AG* 2: 26

'And now the Day Star from on high begins to shine; and Jesus is the flesh-made messenger to show that light to men.' - *AG* 14: 22

'We call this child the Day Star from on high, for he has come to bring to men a light, the light of life ...' - *AG* 21: 5

'The people were in darkness, knowing not the way; but, lo, they saw the Day Star rise; a light streamed forth; they saw the way of life; they walked therein.

And you are blest beyond all people of the earth today, because you first may see the light, and may become the children of the light.' - *AG* 88: 6-7

'All hail the Day Star form on high! All hail the Christ who ever was, and is and evermore shall be!' - *AG* 146: 4-5

'... the Sun of Righteousness had arisen; he had found the king. - *AG* 29: 28

'And you will see his star arise, and it will grow until it is the full-orbed Sun of Righteousness.' - *AG* 72

'Lamaas said, Behold the Sun of Righteousness! And he confessed his faith in Christ, and followed him.' - *AG* 80: 22

'And Jesus opened up his eyes and said, All hail the rising sun; the coming of the day of righteousness!' - *AG* 172: 35

The Apostles at Pentecost represented the zodiac constellations:
'A brilliant light appeared, and many thought, The building is afire.
Twelve balls, that seemed like balls of fire, fell from heaven - a ball from every sign of all the circle of the heavens, and on the head of each apostle there appeared a flaming ball of fire.
And every ball sent seven tongues of fire toward heaven, and each apostle spoke in seven dialects of earth.' - *AG* 182: 5-7

The Christ will return during the Age of Aquarius:
'And signs that men have never seen will then appear in heaven and earth; in sun, and moon, and stars...the Prince of Peace will stand above the clouds of heaven and say again: Peace, peace on earth; good will to men; and every man will throw away his sword, and nations will learn war no more. And then **the man who bears the pitcher** will

walk forth across an arc of heaven; the sign and signet of
the son of man will stand forth in the eastern sky.' - *AG* 157

The Heavens tell a story to teach us lessons:
'But all things teach; each has a time and season for its
own. The sun, the moon have lessons of their own for
men; but each one teaches at the appointed time.
The lessons of the sun fall down on human hearts like
withered leaves upon a stream, if given in the season of
the moon; and so with lessons of the moon and all the
stars.' - *AG* 9: 3-4

'Behold the Sun! It manifests the power of God who
speaks to us through sun and moon and stars . . .' - *AG* 12:2

*The Immortal Spirits, the Elohim and the Cherubim and Seraphim
watch over us:*
'But man will full regain his lost estate, his heritage; but
he must do it in a conflict that cannot be told in words.
Yea, he must suffer trials and temptations manifold; but
let him know that cherubim and seraphim that rule the
stations of the sun, and spirits of the mighty God who
rule the solar stars are his protectors and his guides, and
they will lead to victory.' - *AG, Man*

'...and Zarathustra said, The greatest of the Spirits standing near the throne is the Ahura Mazda, who manifests in
brightness of the sun.' - *AG* 10: 23-24

Abram (Abraham) and the Zoroastrian Magi studied the stars:
'This is the cradle-land of the initiate; all secret things be-
long to Egypt land; and this is why the masters come. In
Zoan Abram taught his science of the stars, and in that
sacred temple over there he learned the wisdom of the
wise.' - *AG* 10: 12-1

'And Persia is the magian land where live the priests who
saw the star arise to mark the place where Mary's son was
born, and were the first to greet him as the Prince of
Peace.' - *AG* 10: 26

IX. The Seven Archangels

The Seven Archangels are direct expansions of the Seven Mighty Elohim into the Angelic Plane; therefore, they are the Archangelic Aspects of the Seven Elohim and have masculine and feminine aspects. Many are well known to most people, others are well known in Christian tradition. Levi in his book SC, Pp. 32-33, lists them and says "every one can be traced to its parentage in the Septonate (the Elohim)." Levi lists their names as: Cassiel, Zadkiel, Michael, Raphael, Gabriel, Sammael and Uriel. In Angelology, Cassiel is another name for Jophiel, and Sammael is another name for Chamuel. The feminine Aspects of the Archangels are associated with Virtues and holy personages, five are emphasized that are referenced in the AG: Christine, Faith, Mary, Hope, and Grace. They are often referred to as "a man" or "the semblance of man" in the Bible and the AG, and are often also referred to as "messengers." The word 'angel' means 'messenger.'

The following is a closer study of the Archangelic Aspects:

Michael - Archangel Michael is an Aspect of the Elohim Hercules. He is mentioned by name several times in *Daniel, Jude, and Revelation*. He appeared unto Joshua as the **Captain of the Lord's Host:**

'And it came to pass, when Joshua was by Jericho, that he lifted up his eyes and looked, and, behold, there stood a man over against him with his sword drawn in his hand: and Joshua went unto him, and said unto him, Art thou for us, or for our adversaries?

And he said, Nay; but as Captain of the host of the LORD am I now come. And Joshua fell on his face to the earth, and did worship, and said unto him, What saith my Lord unto his servant?

And the Captain of the LORD's host said unto Joshua, Loose thy shoe from off thy foot; for the place whereon thou standest is holy. And Joshua did so.' - *Joshua* 5: 13-15 *KJV*

Archangel Michael, slayer of the dragon in *Revelation* has always remained the great defender of the faithful. He is said to wield the Sword of Blue Fire and Flame which destroys discord, evil, karma and negativity. Michael is also referred to as the **Prince of Angels.**

The feminine aspect of Archangel Michael is **Faith,** who represents the Virtue of Faith referenced throughout the *AG*. She is mentioned in *The AG* as leading religious worship in ancient times in Babylon, but left as Religion became more and more corrupt:

'Once **Faith** walked forth in Babylon; and she was bright and fair; but she was clothed in such white robes that men became afraid of her. And every wheel began to turn, and Doubt made war on her, and drove her from the land; and she came back no more.' - *AG* 57: 2-3

Archangel Michael and Faith led all of the Spirits of mankind to embodiment into the Realm of Soul and unto Paradise or the Garden of Eden. Archangel Michael and Faith are of the Blue Ray and command the Blue Flame Angels of Faith, Power and Protection.

Mary, mother of Jesus - Mary is the feminine aspect of the Elohim Cyclopea. **Archangel Raphael**, the Angel of Healing, is her masculine aspect. [8]

Mary manifested as the mother of Jesus and because she perfectly followed the Will of God, she was given the title **Queen of Angels** after her Ascension. Mary is an Ascended Lady Master. She is referred to as **Mother Mary**, as not only being the mother of Jesus, but as being the mother of the faithful, the New Creation, the Kingdom of Heaven. She has represented the Holy Breath (Spirit), the Mother God, the Goddess Wisdom for the Christian dispensation, where the Mother God was previously suppressed, forgotten, unknown and not perfectly revealed until now by the Aquarian Christine Church.

Mother Mary has always been associated with healing waters, she is a directress of the Aqua and Emerald Green Ray and commands the Aqua Flame Angels of Healing,

Music, Science and Supply (Providence).

Gabriel - Archangel **Gabriel** is the Hero par excellence and is an Aspect of the Elohim of Purity.

He is mentioned in *Daniel* and *Luke*. He announced the births of John the Harbinger (the Baptist) and Jesus the Christ in *AG* 2; and is identified as the Angel who rolled the stone away from the tomb of Jesus, thus he is **The Angel of the Resurrection**; *Matthew* 28 & *AG* 172:

'Again, and this was just before the sun arose, the heavens blazed with light, a distant thunder seemed to herald forth a coming storm; And then the earth began to quake and in the rays of light they saw a form descend from heaven. They said, Behold an angel comes. And then they heard again, Adon Mashich Cumi. And then the white-robed form tramped on the Roman seal and then he tore it into shreds; he took the mighty stone in hand as though it were a pebble from the brook, and cast it to the side. And Jesus opened up his eyes and said, All hail the rising sun; the coming of the day of righteousness!' - *AG* 172: 31-35

Archangel Gabriel is also known as **Graphael, The Keeper of the Scrolls**, the Akashic Records, the Book of Life. [9] He is **The Recording Angel** and the Scrolls of Graphael are mentioned in *AG* 158. Graphiel (Gabriel) is also identified with "the Man Clothed in Linen" in *Ezekiel*.

The feminine Aspect is **Hope**, who bestows the virtue of Hope, referenced in *AG* 20:20; 45: 19. Hope is the **Spirit of the Resurrection**. Archangel Gabriel and Hope are of the White Ray and command the White Flame Angels of Hope, Purity, the Resurrection and the Ascension. [10]

Uriel - Archangel Uriel is an Aspect of the Elohim of Peace. He is referred to as the **Messenger of Peace** in *The AG* that announced the birth of Jesus:

'And when the child of promise came, a man in snow-white robe appeared to them, and they fell back in fear. The man stood forth and said, Fear not! behold I bring you joyful news. At midnight in a cave in Bethlehem was born the prophet and the king that you have long been waiting for.' - *AG* 3: 10-11

'He went up to the hills where more than thirty years before the shepherds watched their flocks and heard **the messenger of peace** exclaim: At midnight in a cave in Bethlehem the Prince of Peace is born.' - *AG* 76: 3-4

'And then again the hills of Bethlehem were clothed with light, again **the messenger** exclaimed,

Peace, peace on earth, good will to men.' - *AG* 76: 23-24

The feminine aspect is **Grace** who bestows the virtue of Divine Grace, referenced throughout the *AG*. She overshadowed Mary, when she was embodied as the mother of Jesus and filled her with the virtue of Grace. Archangel Uriel and Grace are of the Purple and Gold Ray and command the Purple Flame Angels of Grace,

Peace, and Tranquility.

Christine - The **Angel of Illumination** is Christine, a feminine Aspect of the Elohim Cassiopeia. Her masculine aspect is Archangel Jophiel, also known as Cassiel. Christine represents illumination and wisdom. The name Christine reflects the name of the Church, the sincere believer, a state of Consciousness and the Kingdom of Heaven. She is **The Christine Angel, The Angel of Christine Consciousness** and is directress of the Yellow Ray and commands the Golden Flame Angels of Illumination, which inspire us and protect the Church and sincere believers.

Zadkiel - Archangel Zadkiel is an Aspect of the Elohim Arcturus and represents Justice and Divine Command. Zadkiel is the **Angel of Mercy** who Levi refers to in his poem *Illumination*. Archangel Zadkiel is of the Violet Ray and bestows the Violet Flame that consumes karma and all negativity and commands the Violet Flame Angels of Transmutation, Mercy and Justice.

The Angel of Love - The masculine Aspect of the Elohim Orion is Archangel Chamuel, also known as Sammael, and is the Angel of Love. He represents the virtues of Divine Love and Compassion. The Angel of Love was the **Angel of Gethsemane** who strengthened Jesus during his Agony in the Garden mentioned in *Luke*

22: 43. [11] The Angel of Love is of the soft Pink Ray and commands the Pink and Lavender Flame Angels of Compassion and Love.

Faith, Hope and the Angel of Love, represent the Three Great Virtues in *AG* 20: 20. They form a Trinity of Divine Virtue. The greatest of these Virtues is Love.

X. The Five Christine Commands

Five basic commands or commandments are given by Jesus, including one that is to keep the Ten Commandments given by God to Moses.

1. The Golden Chord

And Jesus said, I do not see a greatest of the Ten Commands. I see a golden cord that runs through all the Ten Commands that binds them fast and makes them one.

The cord is love, and it belongs to every word of all the Ten Commands.

If one is full of love, he can do nothing else than worship God; for God is love.

If one is full of love, he cannot kill; he cannot falsely testify; he cannot covet; can do naught but honour God and man.

If one is full of love he does not need commands of any kind. - *AG* 17: 3-8

2. The Golden Rule

Do unto other men what you would have them do to you.

- *AG* 68: 20

Do unto others as you would have them do unto you. - *AG* 97: 29

3. **The Diamond Rule**

Whoever is not kind to every form of life - to man, to beast, to bird, and creeping thing - cannot expect the blessings of the Holy one; for as we give, so God will give to us. - *AG* 74: 23-24

What you would have your God give unto you, give unto men. The measure of your worth lies in your service unto men. - *AG* 101:10

4. **The Greatest Command**

Hear O Israel, the Lord our God is one; and you shall love the lord your God with all your heart, with all your mind, with all your soul, with all your strength;
And you shall love your neighbor as yourself. - *AG* 155: 27-28

5. **The New Command**

I give you a new command: As I love you and give my life for you, so shall you love the world, and give your life to save the world.
Love one another as you love yourselves, and then the world will know you are the sons of God, disciples of the son of man whom God has glorified. - *AG* 161: 4-5

The controversial theological point is that rules are different for every person, there are always mitigating circumstances:

'When men defy their consciences and listen not to what they say, the heart is grieved and they become unfitted for the work of life; and thus they sin.

The conscience may be taught. One man may do in conscience what another cannot do.

What is a sin for me to do may not be sin for you to do. The place you occupy upon the way of life determines what is sin.

There is no changeless law of good; for good and evil both are judged by other things.' - *AG* 119: 19-22

The Law of Karma is a universal law:

'And Jesus said, **Afflictions all are partial payments on a debt, or debts, that have been made**.

There is a law of recompense that never fails, and it is summarized in that **true rule of life**:

Whatsoever man shall do to any other man some other man will do to him.

In this we find the meaning of the Jewish law, expressed concisely in the words, Tooth for a tooth; life for a life.

He who shall injure any one in thought, or word, or deed, is judged a debtor to the law, and some one else shall, likewise, injure him in thought, or word or deed.

And he who sheds the blood of any man will come

upon the time when his blood shall be shed by man.

Affliction is a prison cell in which a man must stay until he pays his debts unless a master sets him free that he may have a better chance to pay his debts. Affliction is a certain sign that one has debts to pay.' - *AG* 138: 4-10

This is why the Golden Rule is so important to put into practice in one's life and why one should live by the Golden Chord of Love that binds the Ten Commandments.

XI. Ascended Masters

The Ascended Host is the Brotherhood of Ascended Masters. Becoming an Ascended Master is the goal of earthly embodiment as a human being. They are known in the *AG* as the Silent Brotherhood Clothed in Shimmering White and are known in Theosophy as The Great White Brotherhood (white referring to their auras and robes, not their race.) During the 19th and 20th centuries, several Ascended Masters came forth from the Divine Spirit Realm and were prominent in giving Theosophical teaching and instruction, thereby bringing greater Enlightenment to the world.

Those members of the Ascended Host that are mentioned in the *AG* are referred to as Aquarian Masters. The correlations between the Ascended Masters of Theosophy and the I AM Movement are found in several works, but indispensable in this study are *The Life and Teachings of Jesus and Mary* by A.D.K. Luk and *The Mystical Life of Christ* by the famous Rosicrucian Spencer Lewis.

Ascended Masters are those who have become At-One

with God and are Divine. They are not compelled to embody on the physical plane and are eternally free from the cycle of rebirth. They commune with the righteous seeker and may be called upon to assist us in any constructive way. This is a central teaching of the *AG*. Jesus communed with Ascended Masters and was over-shadowed (watched over and instructed) by a Great Master, the Maitreya; *AG* 40.

Jesus speaks at the Transfiguration:
Heaven and earth are one; masters there and masters here are one. The veil that separates the worlds is but an ether veil. For those who purify their hearts by faith the veil is rolled aside, and they can see and know that death is an illusive thing. - *AG* 129

The Great Work of the Ascended Masters:
The great work of masters is to restore the heritage of man; to return him to his estate he lost, when he will live again upon the ethers of his native plane. - *AG* 32

The following names and biographical sketches are derived from Theosophy (Levi was a Theosophist) and are esoteric in nature. They are the names of the Aquarian Masters in their Ascended State.

Four of the Cherubim are Ascended Masters, who volunteered to manifest on earth in able to instruct us in raising the body in the Resurrection and Ascension processes. They did not take on the cycle of human

76

embodiment or reincarnation, but manifested on this plane to be a focus of Great Spiritual Power. They are represented symbolically as "the four living creatures" in *Ezekiel* and *Revelation*. The four heads of a ram, a bull, a man and an eagle are emblems referring to the zodiac, each are associated emblematically with a ram or lamb, a bull or ox and an eagle or hawk in various religious and esoteric traditions throughout history. The four Cherubim are:

Maha Chohan (mah - choh - hahn)- The Maha Chohan means "great spirit or lord" and is the Cherubic Aspect of the Elohim Cassiopeia. He was Apollonius of Tyana and is known as Apollo, one of the Seven Sages in the *AG*. [12] The Maha Chohan was also the epic poet Homer of Ancient Greece in an earlier manifest. The Maha Chohan is the **Representative of the Holy Spirit**, the Mother God, as is his kindred spirit Minerva (Pallas Athena). As such, he serves on all seven Rays, but primarily on the Aqua Ray of Integration and often on the Yellow Ray of Illumination and Wisdom.

Maitreya (my - trey - yah) - He is known in the *AG* as Melchisedec the Christ and manifested as the historical Krishna. Gautama Buddha is an Aspect of the Maitreya. Rama (Rama'sa), also known as the Cosmic Being Neptune is an Aspect of the Maitreya as well and is the Ruler of the element of water, the spirits of water and wave, and the moon and tides; therefore the Maitreya is the **Ruler of water**. The Maitreya is the Cherubic Aspect of Surya, the Elohim of Sirius, who in turn is an Aspect of the Elohim Hercules, known also as Hare Krishna. Krishna and Gautama Buddha are both considered Manifests of Christ. Jesus lived and studied in his temple in India, the Temple Jagganath. Jagganath has served and does serve as both a Hindu temple of Krishna and as a Buddhist temple. Jesus also journeyed to Tibet to study the teaching of Buddha. The Maitreya was the Great Master who overshadowed Jesus. As a Cosmic Being, he is known as **The Cosmic Christ**. Melchisedec is mentioned in *Genesis*, the *Gospels* and *Hebrews*. The Maitreya serves on the Blue Ray of Faith, Power and Protection.

Words of Buddha:
'He is the noble man who is himself what he believes that other men should be.'
'Love will purify the heart of him who is beloved as truly as it purifies the heart of him who loves.' - *AG* 11

Oromasis (ore - oh - mass - iss) - Prince Oromasis is a Cherubim who is the **Ruler of fire**. He is known in the *AG* as Enoch the Christ who Ascended to Heaven in *Genesis*, he later manifested as Zarathustra the founder of Zoroastrianism. [13] Zarathustra or Zoroaster is considered a Manifest of Christ as well. Esoterically and in Theosophy, he is known as Prince

Oromasis, in recognition of him being the Initiate, Prophet, Representative and an Aspect of Ahura Mazda (Ormazd, Ormasdes.) Oromasis also overshadowed Jesus. As a Cosmic Being, he is known as **The Cosmic Zarathustra**. Oromasis is invoked as Director of the Sacred Fire and serves on all seven Rays, but primarily on the Violet Ray, because it is the Power behind the Violet Flame of Transmutation.

Serapis - Known anciently in Egypt as Osiris, he is the kindred Spirit of Liberty (Isis). In the *AG*, Serapis is known as Matheno, Hierophant of the Lodge of the Heavens and Earth of the Silent Brotherhood in the Temples of Sakara, Heliopolis (and Luxor) in Egypt; teacher of John the Baptist (Elijah;) and one of the Seven Sages. [14] Serapis is the **Hierarch of the White Ray** of Purity, Hope, and the Resurrection and the Ascension processes.

Two mighty feminine Spirits embodied to embody the Divine Mother principle on earth and exemplify the holiness of woman unto the children of God. They are Quan Yin, one of the Seraphim and Mother Mary, an Archangel. Mary is known as the Madonna in Christianity and Quan Yin is known as the Buddhist Madonna or Madonna of the East.

Quan Yin - The Buddhist and Taoist **Goddess of Mercy**, Ascended Lady Master Quan Yin, is said to have not taken on the cycle of human embodiment, but manifested on this plane to be a focus of the Mercy of Sanat Kumara and the Mother God. Upon Her Ascension and returning to Her Heavenly State, she heard the cries of humanity and was so moved by Divine Compassion that she refused to enter Heaven unless all mankind could find salvation, so great was her love for the children of God. Quan Yin was the former Hierarch of the Violet Ray upon which she still serves, and is the **Ruler of the Age of Aquarius**, the Age of the Holy Spirit, the Mother God.

Beloved Mary - Mary manifested in order to be Jesus' mother who instructed and inspired him in his early childhood. Many believe she was a virgin when she conceived and is called the Virgin Mary in the Christian dispensation. She remained one of the most faithful disciples, stood by the Cross and was the first person to witness the Resurrection. She has been known as the **Queen of Angels** since her Ascension.

Mother Mary serves on the Aqua Ray of Healing, Science and Supply (Providence).

The Aquarian Angelis:
'Hail Mary, full of Grace,
The Lord is with thee.
Blessed art thou amongst women.' - *Luke* 1:28, KJV

'Hail Mary, hail! Once Blessed in the Name of God;
Twice Blessed in the Name of Holy Breath;
Thrice Blessed in the Name of Christ; for thou art
worthy.' - *AG* 2:15

The following twelve Aquarian Masters took embodiment and are originally of the plane of Mankind and are not of the plane of Cherubim, Seraphim or Angels. Like us, they too had to take on negative karma and had to achieve the Victory of the Ascension through many earthly embodiments; therefore, they achieved more in that they suffered in the physical plane as most of us have and do as well.

Lord Jesus the Christ - In Aquarian Christine teachings Jesus, the Christine Master is the Hierarch of the Brotherhood of Aquarian Masters. This teaching is found in all of Levi Dowling's work and is found in *Twelve Lessons in Truth - Aum* (1931) by Julianna McKee which is endorsed by Levi's son Leo W. Dowling. Before embodying as Jesus of Nazareth, Jesus embodied as Abel, the son of Adam (Son of Man, Son of Manu) and returned as Seth. Seth was considered by many ancients to be a Manifest of Christ.

Jesus was the **Manifest of Christ, God the Son** and was the **Manifest of Love**, which refers to him being the Manifest of **Sananda**, an Aspect of Orion, the Elohim of Love. Lord Jesus was the Hierarch for the Piscean Age,

81

the Christian dispensation. As the Prince of Peace, he is the **Hierarch of the Purple Ray and Gold Ray** of Grace and Peace. Jesus also serves as co-Hierarch of the soft Pink Ray of Love with Ascended Lady Master Nada. Jesus is different from Enoch the Christ (Oromasis the Cosmic Zarathustra) and from Melchisedec the Christ (Maitreya the Cosmic Christ), in that he died and Resurrected his body and then Ascended into Heaven. He truly is, as He said, The Resurrection and The Life.

Nada (nah - duh) - The kindred soul of Jesus, the disciple who sang sacred songs, stood by the Cross and was the second witness to the Resurrection. Known as Miriam in the *AG* she was an Adept in the Temple of the Silent Brotherhood in Heliopolis in Egypt, where she was the Maiden of Divine Love in the Initiations of the Seven Degrees that Jesus achieved his Victory and title of Christ. Miriam was one of "The Three Marys at the Tomb;" the others being Mary Magdalene and Mother Mary.

She is known esoterically as The Miriam Nada and represents the **Bride of Christ**, which is the Kingdom of Heaven, the Heavenly City of New Jerusalem and the Church in *Revelation*. Nada was the **Manifest of the Dawn of Peace and Righteousness**, an Aspect of the Elohim of Peace (Goddess of the Dawn and Peace).

Miriam is the same as Mary (Maria or Miriam) the Jewess of history, who later resided in Alexandria, Egypt, where she established and led the Gnostic Christine

Church and was the great inventor of the still and the bain-marie (water-bath; double boiler) and celebrated lady master of alchemy. Esoteric tradition and the *AG* teach that she was the reembodiment of Miriam the Prophetess and sister of Moses, who watched over him in the bull-rushes when he was cast adrift in the Nile in a basket and became the celebrated singer and composer of songs of praise. Ascended Lady Master Nada is the **Hierarch of the Pink Ray** of Love and is a co-Hierarch of the Purple Ray and Gold Ray of Grace and Peace serving under Jesus the Christ.

John the Beloved - The only Apostle that stood by the Cross. He was one of the Evangelists and wrote Revelation. He is also known as the Beloved Disciple and St. John the Divine. John is the only Apostle who Ascended at the end of that embodiment. John the Beloved serves on the soft Pink Ray of Love and on the Purple and Gold Ray of Mercy and Peace.

Elijah - After Ascending in a Fiery Chariot, the prophet Elijah later embodied as John the Harbinger (John the Baptist.) He appeared after his martyrdom is the Ascended State with Moses beside Jesus at the Transfiguration. He was the **Manifest of Purity**, the Elohim of Purity. Ascended Master Elijah serves on the White Ray of Hope, Purity and the Resurrection.

Moses - founder of Judaism and the first person to whom God revealed His Sacred Name, *JAHHEVAHE*, which means "I AM that I AM." He appeared in the Ascended Master State with Elijah beside Jesus at the Transfiguration. Moses was the Hierarch for the Arian Age or Age of Aries, the Age of the Judaic dispensation and was the former Hierarch of the Green (Aqua) Ray of Healing, Music, Science and Supply upon which he still serves.

Djwal Kul (jew - all - cool) - Known as Kaspar, one of the three Magi and also one of the Seven Sages in the *AG*. Kaspar means "treasure master" and Djwal Kul means "the cool flame." He is the **Hierarch of the Aqua Ray** and the bearer of the Healing Aqua Flame.

Morya (more - ree - uh) - He was the patriarch Abraham, whose Spiritual Teacher was Melchisedec the Christ, the Maitreya. Through this initiation into the Melchisedec Priesthood, Abraham became the Spiritual Father of the three great Monotheistic religions Judaism, Christianity and Islam. Morya later embodied as Melzone (mell - zone - nay) known also as Melchior, one of the three Magi in the *AG*. He is the **Hierarch of the Blue Ray** of Faith, Power and Will serving under the Divine Director.

Divine Director - The Great Divine Director is

known as **The Manu** or progenitor of mankind, Whose Aspects embodied as **Adam** and **Noah**. In the *AG*, he is called **Vidyapati** (vee - juh - paw - duh), one of the Seven Sages and in India appeared unto Jesus in the Ascended Master state to instruct him in spiritual needs of mankind for the Piscean Age. The Divine Director serves on the Blue Ray of Faith, Power and Will and directs or oversees human embodiments.

Saint Germain - Jesus' father **Joseph** the carpenter who later returned in the Ascended Master State as the mysterious, miracle worker the Count of Saint Germain. He founded many lodges of secret societies. Saint Germain means "holy brother." Prior to embodying as Joseph, the husband of Mary, he was embodied as the Prophet Samuel. He is the bearer of the teachings about the Violet Flame, which by the Grace of God dissolves all discord, karma and negativity. He is the **Hierarch of the Violet Ray** and the **Hierarch of the Age of Aquarius**, serving under the Cosmic Being Quan Yin.

Lanto - He appeared in the Ascended Master State unto Jesus in Tibet and is known as Meng-Ste (ming - zay) one of the Seven Sages in the *AG*. He was the great Chinese philosophers Laotan (Lao-Tzu) and Mencius in earlier embodiments. Lanto is the **Hierarch of the Yellow Ray** of Illumination and Wisdom serving under Kuthumi.

Kuthumi (koo - too - mee) - Known as Zara (czar - uh) also known as Balthasar, one of the three Magi in the *AG*. He was Pythagoras in an earlier embodiment and later embodied as Saint Francis, patron of animals. Kuthumi also assists animals, especially pets in a peaceful passing. Kuthumi serves as **The World Teacher** of Spiritual Truth and is the former Hierarch of the Yellow Ray of Illumination and Wisdom upon which he still serves.

Chananda (shah - nahn - duh) - The Spiritual Head of the Silent Brotherhood (Great White Brotherhood) in India and serving on the **Darjeeling Council** in the Etheric Realm. He is known as Lamaas (la - moss) in the *AG* and was Jesus friend during his travels in India and even traveled to Judea to witness Jesus' Ministry. [15] Jesus referred to him as "The Star of India"; *AG* 80.

XII. Genesis, the Antedeluvian Ages

The Triune God of the Universe, the Father, Mother and Christ the Son decided that the Seven Mighty Elohim should create our solar system and the Three Realms of Spirit, Soul and Manifest (material existence or dense matter). From out of the vastness of the Universe, Seven Great Lifestreams, who are Aspects of the Seven Great Elohim, volunteered to form our solar system. The first and greatest of these Beings to volunteer was Sanat Kumara, an Aspect of the Elohim of Arcturus, the Elohim closest to the Throne of the Triune God. Sanat Kumara, the Eternal Youth is also known as Ahura Mazda, the Wise Lord and He is the Ancient of Days. Sanat Kumara volunteered to serve our solar system as the direct representative of Jehovah, God the Father. Sanat Kumara had such a magnificent Position of Exceedingly Divine Glory, that his volunteering to direct the creation of this solar system is called The Great Sacrifice. Other Aspects of the Elohim volunteered and joined Sanat Kumara: Helios became our Solar Ruler; Astrea purified the elements; the Great Silent

Watcher came to oversee the earth; the Goddess of the Dawn came to create atmospheres, etc.. Each created a different plane of existence for our planet: cherubim, angels, mankind, animals, plants, elements and microscopic and nuclear worlds.

Surya came from Sirius and represented Hercules, the Strength of Christ (Hare Krishna). Surya the Maitreya, the Cosmic Christ was instrumental in creating mankind and the Manifest of Surya was the Manu, the Great Divine Director, whose masculine and feminine aspects we would translate as Adam and Eve. Surya the Maitreya is known as the Lord God who walked in the Garden of Eden in *Genesis* 2-3. Hercules is associated with the Garden of the Hesperides and the tree which bore the golden apples, which is analogous to or mythically echoes the Garden of Eden, the Tree of Life and the Tree of the Knowledge of Good and Evil. Hercules' feminine Aspect was referred to as Hebe, the cup bearer of the divine nectar and the bearer of the feast of divine ambrosia. Hebe is a direct cognate to Eve. In the Spirit Realm, the first man Adam Kadmon, the Adi-Manu or primordial Manu, came forth and was led by Archangel Michael and Faith into the Realm of Soul and became the Adam of Paradise, the Garden of Eden. Adam, the father or progenitor of all mankind, is called the Manu and is known as **the Ascended Master the Great Divine Director**. Other Spirits of men and women followed Archangel Michael, Faith and the Divine Director into the Realm of Soul.

Men and women began to be pulled by their material desires away from focusing on the Source of their Life, God the I AM. Thus, by directing their attention towards more and more imperfection, they "fell" into the Realm of Manifest, our current dimension or realm of existence. A Cherubim, one of Surya the Maitreya's Aspects, guarded us from returning into the Realm of Soul and Spirit after our fall. We fell into a negative plane where there is gradual evolution overlong periods time from primordial and primitive states of being coupled by ignorance, endless rounds of physical embodiment or reincarnation, survival of the fittest, and carnivorous behavior through slaughter. These negative conditions come with the territory, along with evil and sin. However, Archangel Michael vowed to be the Eternal Protector of the Righteous and other angels, the Cherubim and Seraphim also promised to help us regain our lost estate.

Adam had two sons, Cain and Abel. Abel was a holy and righteous individual and was murdered by Cain, his own brother. Abel was an earlier embodiment of the **Ascended Master Beloved Jesus the Christ**. Abel transmigrated and returned unto his parents in re-embodiment as Seth, but now he came as the Manifest of Christ. [16] Seth means "Anointed," which means Messiah or Christ. Transmigration is not reincarnation. Transmigration means one re-embodies in a very short period of time; reincarnation means one travels through various levels of spiritual evolution and cleansing before re-embodying, sometimes many centuries later.

Several generations after Seth the Christ lived, **Enoch** was born. Enoch was a Cherubim and also was the Manifest of Christ. Enoch was the Messenger and Prophet of the Ancient of Days, Ahura Mazda or Sanat Kumara, the Aspect of the Elohim Arcturus unto this solar system and the earth. In recognition of Enoch being the Messenger, Prophet and Manifest of Ahura Mazda, he is known as **the Ascended Master Prince Oromasis**, the Ruler of the spirits of fire. Enoch the Christ Ascended publicly and many of his followers with him.

Then, centuries later, Rama (Rama'sa), the Ruler of the spirits of water, a Cherubic Aspect of **the Maitreya** manifested as a great ruler named Poseidon (Neptune), who ruled his people even after he made the Ascension in his Ascended Master State. Afterwards, many centuries later, the Maitreya returned as **Krishna**, who is said to have been born of a virgin, Wise Men followed a great star and brought gifts to the holy child. [17] Krishna later became a great ruler and military leader. Krishna was a Manifest of Christ and returned to the Ascended State.

Around this time humans were becoming more and more corrupt. In Babylon, Archangel Faith led worship at the Shrine of the Temple of the Unseen God, but men became so evil they made war against her. Archangel Faith withdrew from the world and mankind because of this; it is said that Astrea, the Elohim of Purity withdrew, as well. The Mother God also withdrew a portion of Herself from the world and mankind and thus, being the Holy Breath, the Very Breath of Life, the life-span of everything living on earth was greatly reduced. The feminine Divine Energies withdrew and females were vilified by mankind and it has taken thousands of years for them to return unto the earth and to commune with mankind.

It was decided by Heavenly Courts that because of their corrupt nature, mankind must be destroyed by a Great Flood, the Great Cataclysm. If mankind were to begin again afterwards, an aspect of the Manu must re-embody. So, another aspect of **the Great Divine Director**, the Manu re-embodied as Noah.

XIII. The Patriarchs, the Arian Age

Many centuries later, Abraham was born and was a great and holy man. Abraham is known as the Ascended Master Morya. The AG teaches that it was during Morya's embodiment as Abraham that he was initiated into the mysteries of Egypt. Esoteric teachings record that while in Egypt, he also was an Initiate of the Silent Brotherhood (the Great White Brotherhood), became a Living Unascended Master and was the founder of the teaching of Baptism in water to purify the soul. [18] Abraham's spiritual teacher and priest was the Maitreya who manifested then as Melchisedec the Christ. They most probably first met in Egypt, where Melchisedec was crowned by the kings of Egypt. The Maitreya simply manifested from the Ascended State as a Living Ascended Master, Melchisedec. The book of Hebrews tells us: he was not born and did not die, but simply returned to the Ascended State. Melchisedec was the King and High Priest of Salem and was the Prince of Peace. Abraham's faith was tested and he was going to sacrifice his son Isaac on Mt. Moriah in Salem (Salim), when suddenly Archangel Zadkiel, the Angel of Mercy stopped him. Zadkiel, the Angel of the Lord, thus revealed the unacceptability of human sacrifice and really all blood sacrifices. [19] Salem is modern day Jerusalem and Mt. Moriah is the Temple of the Mount where the Solomon's temple of Jerusalem once stood.

XIV. Exodus

Not long afterwards, a great leader and prophet was born named Moses. His sister was Miriam the Prophetess and is known as the Ascended Lady Master Nada. Nada means the "voice of the Silence (Nirvana)." During the slaughter of the Hebrew male children under the orders of the Pharaoh, Miriam took her baby brother Moses hidden in a basket and guided him in the water to where the Princess of Egypt would find him and she adopted him as her son and he became part of the royal household and Prince of Egypt.

Later, Moses was exiled and had a religious experience where the Sacred Name of God, the Omnific Word, *JAHHEVAHE* was revealed to him by Archangel Michael who manifested unto Moses in a burning bush. The Sacred Name is the same in meaning and as the "I AM that I AM" and embodies the same Divine Vibration as the English words I AM, but in a more dynamic way. Through the Power of the Omnific Word, Moses was able to free his people and lead them to the Promised

Land. Miriam the Prophetess composed several hymns of Victory during the Exodus. Moses is an Ascended Master and was seen beside Jesus at the Transfiguration. Ascended Master Moses was the Hierarch of the Arian Age (Age of Aries).

Archangel Michael appeared again unto Joshua during a time of battle. Archangel Michael revealed that he was the Captain of the Lord's Host.

XV. The Prophets

During the years surrounding the foundation of Israel, the prophet Samuel embodied and is known as the Ascended Master Saint Germain. [20] After Samuel passed on at an old age, he transmigrated and re-embodied as Hiram Abiff, the Master Mason and builder of the Temple of Solomon, of whom the Freemasonic traditions are based. Some ancient Hebrew esoteric teachings record the belief that Hiram was believed to have been murdered for not revealing the Sacred Name of God, but through the Power of his knowledge of the Sacred Name (JAHHEVAHE), and his faithfulness in guarding the sacredness of the Omnific Word, he Resurrected and Ascended into Heaven.

Around a hundred years later, **Elijah** embodied as the great prophet and religious reformer of Israel. He Ascended into Heaven in a fiery chariot.

After a period of time, **Prince Oromasis**, the Messenger and Prophet of Ahura Mazda, Sanat Kumara, manifested in Persia as the prophet **Zarathustra**, the founder of Zoroastrianism. Zarathustra was the Manifest of Christ and taught the use of the Sacred Fire. It is said he was born of a virgin and Ascended into Heaven while being martyred at the altar in a temple. [21]

Not long afterwards, an Aspect of **the Maitreya** manifested in India as **Gautama Buddha,** the founder of Buddhism. Although an Aspect of the Maitreya, Buddha is considered to be a different lifestream. Gautama Buddha was the Manifest of Christ and is said to have been born of a virgin, a great star appeared and Wise Men visited the child bearing gifts. [22] Buddha preached his reformative teachings and entered the Silence (Nirvana) while meditating under a tree and then Ascended.

A few years later, **Pythagoras** the great mathematician, scientist, music theorist and mystic embodied in Greece and is said to have born of a virgin. He is known as **the Ascended Master Kuthumi.** [23] He discovered the Pythagorean theorem and that the musical scale is derived mathematically.

Around the time of Pythagoras, a philosopher was born in China, **Lao Tan (Lao Tzu).** Lao Tan was the Duke of Chou, the founder of Taoism, is said to have born of a virgin and was an earlier embodiment of **the Ascended Master Lanto.** [24]

A century after that, Lanto re-embodied in China as the Confucian philosopher and reformist **Mencius (Meng-Ste)** and because of this he is called the Second Sage Duke of Chou.

About three hundred years before the birth of Jesus

the Christ, the Cherubim known as **the Ascended Master Serapis** manifested as **Manetho,** the Egyptian historian and Hierophant of the Temple of Heliopolis. Most of what we know today of ancient Egypt is owed to Manetho.

XVI. The Dawn of Christianity, the Piscean Age

The parents of Mary, the mother of Jesus, were Joachim and Anna, an extremely pious and righteous couple. Mary was of the Angelic Plane, the feminine Aspect of Archangel Raphael and manifested in order to bear Jesus the Christ. Archangel Gabriel announced the birth of Mary first to Joachim and then unto Anna. Mary was brought up in the temple as a weaver of the sacred purple used as curtains and table coverings in temple ritual and decoration. Saint Germain was embodied then as Joseph, a carpenter and a devout Essene. Joseph, being an Essene was a member of the Silent Brotherhood, the Great White Brotherhood and a great initiate within its ranks. His spiritual teacher was the Great Divine Director, Vidyapati who was an Ascended Master whose main focus was in a retreat in far away India. [25] During that embodiment, Joseph was overshadowed by Archangel Zadkiel. [26] When it was time to choose suitors for Mary, the candidates placed there staffs down in the temple and Joseph's burst into bloom and an almond blossom or lily miraculously sprouted forth. A dove also descended and landed on the staff, a sign of the Holy Spirit, the Mother Goddess approving Joseph as father to Jesus.

Archangel Gabriel then went unto Mary's kinsmen, Zacharias and Elizabeth and announced the birth of **John** the Baptist, the Harbinger. It was important that Gabriel announce John's birth, and Gabriel is said to bring the Spirit of **Elijah,** an Ascended Master unto Elizabeth to be re-embodied. John being the Manifest of the Elohim of Purity, it was also necessary for Gabriel to bring the Spirit of Elijah, because Gabriel is the Archangel Aspect of the Elohim of Purity.

Not long after this, Archangel Gabriel came unto Mary and announced the birth of Jesus. Gabriel saluted her as full of Grace. Grace is not only a virtue, but a feeling and the feminine Aspect of Archangel Uriel and the Archangelic Aspect of the Elohim of Peace, associated with the Dawn. [27] It was necessary that Mary be filled with Divine Grace, because Jesus the Christ was the Manifest of the Elohim of Peace and that is why he is known as the Prince of Peace. Archangel Gabriel also explained to Mary that 'the Holy Ghost (the Mother God) shall come upon thee, and the Power of the Highest (Jehovah, the Father God) shall overshadow thee; therefore also that holy thing that shall be born of thee shall be called the Son of God (Christ).' - *Luke* 1: 35, *KJV* If one accepts the Virgin Birth of Jesus, one may interpret this to mean that the primordial Birth of Christ that occurred in Heaven, the Spirit Realm of Akasha, when the Father God and Mother God breathed in unison and their only begotten Son, the Christ stood before them, reoccurred on the earth plane through the conduit of Mary's physical body and soul. This would mean Mary who had been filled with the Archangel Grace, then had the Mother God come upon her and fill Her as well, thus serving as a vessel for Her. Mother Mary, Archangel Grace and the Mother God form a Trinity of the Divine Feminine.

John was born July 25th and Jesus was born five months later on Dec. 25th, according to the *AG*. Jesus was born on Dec. 25[th,], in accordance to Cosmic Law. [28] At the birth of Jesus, Archangel Uriel, the Messenger of Peace and legions of Angels of Peace announced the birth of the Prince of Peace unto the shepherds watching their flocks. Three Men in shimmering White Robes were at the birth of Jesus. These were the materialization or apparition of the Spirits of three Living Masters known as Magi: **Melzone** or Melchior, known as **the Ascended Master Morya**; **Zara** or Balthazar, known as **the Ascended Master Kuthumi**; and **Kaspar** (Caspar or Gaspar or Jasper), known as **the Ascended Master Djwal Kul**.

Forty days later on Candlemas, Feb. 2nd, the baby Jesus was presented at the temple and at that time three Magi ambassadors of the three Magi Living Masters arrived bearing gifts. This was during Herod's slaughter of the

Holy Innocents, the Magi would not reveal the where-
abouts of Jesus or John unto Herod and Zacharias would
not reveal their location to Herod's soldiers. Zacharias
was murdered by the altar in the temple for protecting his
son and Jesus, this was a great sacrilege. Zacharias and the
Holy Innocents are the first of the Christine Martyrs.

Jesus worked with his father Joseph as a carpenter.
Joseph as a devout Essene, instructed Jesus in Essene
teachings. It should be noted that many tools of Carpentry
are the same as of Masonry and thus Freemasonry. Joseph
was an earlier embodiment of the Ascended Master Saint
Germain who founded many Masonic and Rosicrucian
lodges.

'...(Jesus) wrought with Joseph as a carpenter.

One day as he was bringing forth the tools for work
he said, These tools remind me of the ones we handle in
the workshop of the mind where things were made of
thought and where we build up character.

We use he square to measure all our lines, to straighten
out the crooked places of the way, and make the corners
of our conduct square.

We use the compass to draw circles round our passions
and desires to keep them in the bounds of righteousness.

We use the axe to cut away the knotty, useless and un-
gainly parts and make the character symmetrical.

We use the hammer to drive home the truth, and
pound it in until it is a part of every part.

We use the plane to smooth the rough, uneven surfaces

of joint, and block, and board that go to build the temple for the truth.

The chisel, line, the plummet and the saw all have their uses in the workshop of the mind.

And then this ladder with its trinity of steps, faith, hope, and love; on it we climb up to the dome of purity in life.

And on the twelve-step ladder we ascend until we reach the pinnacle of that which life is spent to build - the Temple of Perfected Man.'- *AG* 20: 11-21

The Calling of the Apostles James and Jude, the cousins of Lord Jesus, the Christine Master:

'... Jesus was at home, behold, there came his kindred, James and Jude, the sons of Alpheus and Miriam.

And these were men of faith, and they were carpenters of Nazareth.

And Jesus said to them, Behold, for you have toiled with me, and with my father Joseph, building houses for the homes of men. The masters call us now to aid in building homes for souls; homes built without the sound of hammer, axe, or saw; I go, and you may follow me.

And James and Jude exclaimed, Lord, we will follow you.' - *AG* 88: 30-33

Lord Jesus, the Christine Master prophesies his crucifixion; Jesus is The Capstone of the Royal Arch and The Door which it frames:

'Then turning to the priests and scribes he (Jesus) said,

Did not your prophets say, The stone the builders cast away became the capstone of the arch?

You men who pose as men of God ... have stoned and killed the messengers of God, his prophets and his seers, and now you seek to slay his son.' - *AG* 154

XVII. John the Harbinger (John the Baptist)

John studied under Matheno, who was in the Ascended Master State and is the Ascended Master Serapis. Matheno was the Hierarch of the Egyptian lodges and temples of the Great White Brotherhood and an Essene. Thus, John was a Nazarite and an Essene. Nazarites are vowed even while in the womb to never drink alcohol, be vegetarian, to keep an extremely strict diet and never to touch or even look at a corpse or carrion. John is probably the only Nazarite who kept the law of the Nazarites perfectly and Jesus said there was no greater prophet than John. Matheno taught John the importance of his mission as Harbinger of Jesus the Christ and as the founder of the Church of Purity, later to evolve into the Church of Purity and Love, the Christine Church. Entrance into John's Church of Purity was by Water Baptism to symbolize the purification of the soul. - AG 13-15; 61-64

XVIII. Jesus in India

Jesus traveled to India and became friends with a priest named Lamaas, known as the Ascended Master Chananda. He studied for four years at the Temple of Jagganath (the Maitreya), the temple of Krishna and also Buddha.

Jesus studied Ayur Vedic and Pranic healing under Udraka. As he learned and taught, the greatest of Indian masters, **Vidyapati**, known as **the Ascended Master the Great Divine Director** revealed to the Hindu priests the great Power Within Jesus the Christ. Vidyapati means Father Wisdom or Father of Knowledge, the name or title alluding to the fact that he had been Jesus' father as Adam when he was embodied as Abel and Seth. Vidyapati was in the Ascended Master State. [29] Soon afterwards, Jesus was instructed by Vidyapati in the needs of the Piscean Age and of the future Aquarian Age. He instructed him in his purpose in reforming religious beliefs and establishing the Christine Church. - *AG* 21-35; 37

IXX. Jesus in Tibet

Jesus went to study spiritual teachings in Tibet under the great master Meng-Ste, who was in the Ascended Master State. He is the Ascended Master Lanto. - AG 36

XX. Persia

Jesus went to Persia on his way back to Judea and visited the three Magi who brought him gifts at his birth. During this time, the three great Living Masters Melzone, Zara and Kaspar arrived. These three are great Ascended Masters now: Morya, Kuthumi and Djwal Kul. [30] The Seven Magi formed a College of Seven Magi, including Jesus himself. These Zoroastrian priests were exceedingly holy and righteous. Jesus being the Christ was in total At-One-ment with the Maitreya who overshadowed him and Prince Oromasis who had manifested as the prophet Zarathustra, the founder of Zoroastrianism, the Magi's religion. - AG 38-41

XXI. Jesus in Greece

Jesus then journeyed to Greece to study the great minds of Greek thought and visited the Oracle of Delphi; there he met Apollo, the Defender of the Oracle. Apollo, better known as Apollonius of Tyana, was a Cherubim and an Aspect of the Elohim Cassiopeia who manifested to bring great Illumination unto the Greek philosophers and in the further East. Apollo is known as the Ascended Master the Maha Chohan, who represents the Mother God, the Holy Breath. Apollonius is said to have been born of a virgin, traveled to India and to have publicly Ascended, witnessed by his disciples. - AG 44-46 [31]

XXII. Egypt

Jesus passed through the Seven Degrees of the Secret Brotherhood (The Silent Brotherhood, The Great White Brotherhood) at the Temple of Heliopolis (City of the Sun in Greek), the 7th degree was of "The Christ" and in the temple's Purple Room this title was given to him and he became a Master. These degrees and the events of this sacred drama are recorded in AG 47: 9 - 55:12; each degree associated with a different Victory.

1st Degree - Sincerity - Victory over hypocrisy
2nd Degree - Justice - Victory over prejudice
3rd Degree - Faith - Victory over unbelief
4th Degree - Philanthropy - Victory over selfishness
5th Degree - Heroism - Victory over fear
6th Degree - Love Divine - Victory over carnal love
7th Degree - The Christ - Victory over emotion

These degrees and symbolism are analogous to the Masonic, Rosicrucian and Odd Fellowship degrees. The first degree is that of the Initiate. The second thru forth degrees are analogous to the Blue Lodge of Freemasonry and the Subordinate Lodge of the Odd Fellowship. According to H. Spencer Lewis in *The Mystical Life of Jesus*, the 4th Degree of Philanthropy was the pinnacle and hardest test, as it is in Rosicrucianism. The fifth through seventh degrees are analogous to Scottish Rite Freemasonry and is strikingly similar to the Encampment of the Odd Fellowship. In the last two degrees of the Encampment are the Golden Rule and Royal Purple and are uncannily similar in the sixth and seventh degrees that Jesus undertook.

Matheno (Ascended Master Serapis) served as the Hierophant of the Temple of Heliopolis. It is widely understood in esoteric circles that the Hierophant of any lodge, assumes the role of Osiris or Serapis in administering the different degrees. [32]

Lord Jesus the Christine Master speaks of the Seven Degrees of Initiation:
'When I had passed the seven tests in Heliopolis, I consecrated life and all I had, to save the world.' - *AG* 127: 7

John the Harbinger also was a member of the Secret Brotherhood and passed all his degrees attaining to Master in the Temple of Sakara, Egypt. There he was known as the Brother Nazarite and there he lived for eighteen years (*AG* 15:30-31). He was personally instructed by Matheno

(Serapis). Beloved Mary, mother of Jesus, Joseph (Saint Germain), the Apostle Matthias and Miriam (Nada) were also Initiates of the Secret Brotherhood. [33]

It is taught in esoteric circles that Saint Germain was Hiram Abiff, the widow's son who was the great artificer of brass who helped build the Temple of Solomon and on whom the Freemasonry and Rosicrucian traditions are based. [34] This is alluded to in two paralleling verses and chapters in the *AG*, which refer to Jesus' Initiations at the Lodge of the Secret Brotherhood at Heliopolis and a letter to Mary at the time of his father Joseph's passing. The special role Mary played in the Secret Brotherhood is also alluded to in these passages. - *AG* 30: 3-18 & 54: 3-18 (*compare texts*)

XXIII. Seven Sages & the Seven Postulates

The Seven Sages met with Jesus in Egypt to formulate the Seven Postulates that are the basis of the Christine teachings. Matheno (Serapis), Meng-Ste (Lanto) and Vidyapati (Divine Director) were in the Ascended State already at that time. The other four Sages and Jesus were Living Masters. Kaspar (Djwal Kul), Apollo (the Maha Chohan) and Jesus are Ascended Masters now. Meng-Ste (Lanto) was the eldest Sage and presided over this meeting as the chief. The Seven Postulates rests on the Gnosis of the Empire of the Soul.

THE SEVEN POSTULATES - AG 58-60

1st Postulate - Meng-ste (Ascended Master Lanto)

All things are Thought; all Life is Thought Activity.

The multitude of beings are but phases of the One Great Thought made manifest. Lo, God is Thought, and Thought is God.

2ⁿᵈ Postulate - Vidyapati (the Great Divine Director)

Eternal Thought is One; in Essence It is Two - Intelligence and Force; and when They breathe a Child is born; this Child is Love.
And thus the Triune God stands forth, whom men call Father-Mother-Child.
This Triune God is One; but like the One of Light, in Essence He is Seven.
And when the Triune God breathes forth, lo, Seven Spirits stand before His Face; these are Creative Attributes.
Men call them Lesser Gods, and in Their Image they made Man.

3ʳᵈ Postulate - Kaspar (Ascended Master Djwal Kul)

Man was a Thought of God, formed in the Image of the Septonate, clothed in the substances of soul.
And his desires were strong; he sought to manifest on every plane of Life, and for himself he made a body of the ethers of the earthly forms, and so descended to the Plane of Earth.
In this descent he lost his Birthright; lost his Harmony

with God, and made discordant all the notes of Life. Inharmony and evil are the same; so evil is the handiwork of man.

4th Postulate - Ashbina

Seeds do not germinate in light; they do not grow until they find the soil, and hide themselves away from light. Man was evolved a Seed of Everlasting Life; but in the Ethers of the Triune God the Light was far too great for seeds to grow;
And so Man sought the soil of carnal life, and in the darksomeness of earth he found a place where he could germinate and grow.
The seed has taken root and grown full well.
The Tree of human Life is rising from the soil of earthy things, and, under natural Law, is reaching up to Perfect Form.
There are no supernatural acts of God to lift a man from carnal life to Spirit Blessedness; he grows as grows the plant, and in due time is Perfected.
The quality of soul that makes it possible for man to rise to Spirit Life is Purity.

5th Postulate - Apollo (the Maha Chohan)
The soul is drawn to Perfect Light by four white steeds, and these are Will, and Faith, and Helpfulness and Love.

That which one wills to do, he has the Power to do.

A Knowledge of that Power is Faith; and when Faith moves, the soul begins its flight.

A selfish faith leads not to Light. There is no lonely pilgrim on the Way to Light. Men only gain the Heights by helping others gain the Heights.

The steed that leads the Way to Spirit Life is Love; is Pure Unselfish Love.

6th Postulate - Matheno (Ascended Master Serapis)

The Universal Love of which Apollo speaks is Child of Wisdom and of Will Divine, and God has sent It forth to earth in flesh that man may know.

The Universal Love of which the Sages speak, is Christ.

The greatest mystery of all times lies in the Way that Christ lives in the Heart.

Christ cannot live in clammy dens of carnal things. The seven battles must be fought, the Seven Victories won before the carnal things, like fear, and self, emotions and desire, are put away.

When this is done the Christ will take possession of the soul; the work is done, and Man and God are One.

7th Postulate - Philo

A Perfect Man! To bring before the Triune God a

Being such as This was Nature made.

This Consummation is the Highest Revelation of the Mystery of Life.

When all the essences of carnal things have been transmuted into soul, and all the essences of soul have been returned to Holy Breath, and Man is made a Perfect God, the drama of Creation will conclude. And this is all. Amen.

XXIV. Baptism of Jesus & the Temptations

Jesus went unto the followers of John the Harbinger (Elijah) and submitted to be baptized in order to set a pattern for the Baptismal Rite, the rite of initiation for the Christian dispensation. A voice from Heaven was heard saying, "This is my Son, and in him I AM well pleased." Then the Holy Spirit came down in the form of a dove and sat on Jesus Head. Jesus then left and went into the desert to fast for forty days and conquer the lower self and its temptations.

Jesus was able to conquer his lower self by the Three Victories over the Temptations to Demonstrate Power over the substances of Earth, over the Air and over Mankind through Wealth. - *AG* 65

XXV. Ministry of Jesus

Jesus taught the multitudes, healed many and performed countless miracles. John the Harbinger was imprisoned during Jesus' ministry and was sentenced to death and was beheaded. Lamaas (Chananda) journeyed from India to visit Jesus and witness his ministry. [35] During Jesus' ministry he introduced the Christines to Miriam who held the office of prophetess and composed and sang many songs of inspiration.

XXVI. Transfiguration

Jesus took the Inner Circle of Apostles (Peter, James and the Ascended Master John the Beloved) unto a mountain to pray and meditate. While Jesus prayed, the Inner Circle witnessed the Ascended Masters Elijah (the Ascended John the Baptist) and Moses stand on either side of him. They conversed together on many important things and then Jesus was Transfigured before them. - AG 129

XXVII. Holy Week

Jesus arrived in Jerusalem triumphantly on Palm Sunday. He ate the Passover with his disciples on Maundy Thursday and watched the disciples feet and celebrated the Lord's Supper with them. Judas betrayed him, which led Jesus' arrest, trial and being sentenced to death. Jesus went to the Garden of Gethsemane to pray and was comforted by Archangel Chamuel, the Angel of Love. - Luke 22:43

XXVIII. Crucifixion

Jesus was crucified at noon on Good Friday and died at three o'clock in the afternoon. Simon of Cyrene, an African from Libya and Jesus' friend helped him carry his cross to Golgotha. Other disciples who stood by the cross were: Beloved Mary, the mother of Jesus; Miriam (Ascended Lady Master Nada); Mary Magdalene; and the Ascended Master John the Beloved, who was the only Apostle to stay with Jesus through the end. Jesus laid in the tomb thirty-three hours. - AG 165-171

IXXX. Resurrection

At midnight on Easter Sunday, the Resurrection Lord Jesus the Christ began. The words "Adon Mashich Cumi" were spoken by Ascended Masters and Jesus opened his eyes and said "All hail the Rising Sun." Archangel Gabriel broke the seal and rolled the stone away from the garden tomb. [36] Beloved Mary, mother of Jesus was the first of the disciples to witness the Resurrected Jesus. Then Jesus materialized unto Miriam (Ascended Lady Master Nada), then unto Mary Magdalene and unto the Inner Circle of Apostles, Peter, James and Ascended Master John the Beloved.. - AG 172-173

XXX. Materializations of the Resurrected Jesus

After the Resurrection, Jesus appeared to disciples on the road to Emmaus. - AG 174 The following Saturday, he materialized in the Temple unto the Jewish priests. Then on Sunday appeared unto the Apostles and broke bread. This is called Thomas' Easter, because Jesus had the doubting Thomas to touch his wounds from the crucifixion. - AG 177

Jesus made many materializations in different locations unto his disciples, many are not documented. In the *AG*, Jesus made several materializations unto the Living Sages and Masters, there being great emphasis placed on these materializations and the messages which Jesus relayed to them.

Jesus materialized unto the Masters of the East, Vidyapati (the Divine Director), Meng-Ste (Lanto) and Lamaas (Chananda) in India. - *AG* 176: 1-21

Jesus materialized unto the Magi, Melzone (Morya), Zara (Kuthumi) and Kaspar (Djwal Kul) in Persia. - *AG* 176: 22-37

Jesus materialized unto Apollo (the Maha Chohan) and the Silent Brotherhood in Greece. - *AG* 178: 1-15

Jesus materialized before the Brotherhood in the Temple of Heliopolis. - *AG* 178: 30-47

XXXI. Ascension

On a Thursday, the fortieth day after the Resurrection, Jesus Ascended into the Heavenly Spirit Realm. This was witnessed by the Apostles and a multitude of faithful disciples. - AG 180

XXXII. Pentecost, the Day of Christine Power

Pentecost was on a Sunday, the fiftieth day after the Resurrection (Easter) and was the Establishment of the Christine Church which was marked by the Descent of the Holy Breath, the Holy Spirit. The disciples and the Twelve Apostles experienced the Immersion in Light, the Baptism of the Holy Breath and Fire.

The Apostles at Pentecost represented the zodiac constellations:

'A brilliant light appeared, and many thought, The building is afire.

Twelve balls, that seemed like balls of fire, fell from heaven - a ball from every sign of all the circle of the heavens, and on the head of each apostle there appeared a flaming ball of fire.

And every ball sent seven tongues of fire toward heaven, and each apostle spoke in seven dialects of earth.' - *AG* 182: 5-7

According to Eliphas Levi, each apostle is associated with a specific zodiac constellation. [37] The I AM Movement teaches that the seven tongues of fire are the Seven-fold Flame of the Seven Mighty Elohim, which sits above the brow and spreads across the forehead like a crown. The Seven-fold Flame directs the Seven Rays and Flames of the Seven Mighty Elohim.

Sagittarius - James, the son of Alphaeus (the Greater)
Capricorn - Matthew
Aquarius - Jude (Thaddeus)
Pisces - Matthias
Aries - Peter
Taurus - Simon
Gemini - James (the Less)
Cancer - Andrew
Leo - Ascended Master John the Beloved
Virgo - Phillip
Libra - Nathaniel (Bartholomew)
Scorpio - Thomas

XXXIII. The Christine Church

After the Establishment of the Christine Church, John the Beloved took care of Mary, mother of Jesus until her Ascension, wrote The Gospel of John, Epistles and Revelation and later also Ascended.

The Miriam Nada went to Egypt where she was active in establishing the Gnostic Christine communities and making advanced developments in the field of Alchemy.

The Apostle Thomas journeyed to India and established Christine communities there. Many of the Apostles, disciples and other Christines were martyred. Jesus prophesied that the earth would be baptized in blood, meaning the many martyrdoms in his name.

Around a twelve hundred years later, Saint Francis of Assisi embodied to restore the Christine concept of compassion for animals and all living things. Saint Francis was an embodiment of the Ascended Master Kuthumi. [38]

In the 17th through 19th centuries and continuing into 20th and the 21st centuries, the mysterious Ascender Master Saint Germain has materialized unto the Initiated in his Ascended State. He was behind the founding of the modern Freemasonic, Rosicrucian and ultimately the Odd Fellowship. This is in keeping with the esoteric teachings that Saint Germain was Hiram Abiff, upon whom the symbolism and rituals of the Secret Brotherhood are based. He is the basis for and was considered to be the legendary Christian Rosenkreutz, the founder of the Rosicrucians. [39] In the 1930's, the Ascended Master Saint Germain established the I AM Movement and brought the wonderful gift of the knowledge of the Violet Flame unto the earth and its inhabitants, for its Freedom and Ascension.

AQUARIAN CHRISTINE LIGHT:

The Book of Consolation, Devotion, Illumination,
Meditation, Ministry, and Services

The Twenty-five Holy Days

There are twenty-five days considered holy days of the Aquarian Christine Church that memorialize certain events mentioned in the AG and the Holy Bible. Christmas is kept out of ancient tradition starting at midnight as is told in the AG and fixes the Christian calendar, which the Aquarian Christine Church affirms is the most perfect of all calendars. The Feast of the Holy Name of Jesus is the Feast of the Circumcision of Jesus and is New Year's Day, January 1st. In Judaism, newborn male infants are circumcised and given their name on the eighth day. The remnant of foreskin from the circumcised infant forms a ring or circle, which in regards to Jesus the Manifest of Christ or God, his remnant of foreskin represents the perpetual cycle of time or rather Eternity.

The Seven Great Christine Feasts

Remembrance Day - Thursday evenings
'On Thursday morning Jesus called to him the twelve disciples, and he said to them, This is God's remembrance day, and we will eat the paschal supper all alone. - *AG* 160: 1

Resurrection Day of Victory - Sundays
'At midnight all was well, but suddenly the tomb became a blaze of light.' - *AG* 172: 7

'So in the morning of the first day of the week they hastened to the tomb with spices to further embalm the Lord. But when they reached the tomb...they found an empty tomb...' - *AG* 173: 4-6

'Towards the evening of the resurrection day ...' - *AG* 174: 1

'The evening of the resurrection day had come...' - *AG* 175: 1 (One week later, Sunday is still referred to as the Resurrection Day.)

Maundy Thursday - Feast of the Remembrance; service in evening - *AG* 160

Easter - Resurrection Sunday - AG 172-173

Ascension Thursday - Feast of the Ascension -
'And Jesus stood apart and raised his hands and said,
The benedictions of the Holy Ones, of the Almighty God, and of the Holy Breath, of Christ the love of God made manifest, will rest upon you all the way till you shall rise and sit with me upon the throne of power.
And then they saw him rise upon the wings of light; a wreath encircled him about; and then they saw his form

no more.' - *AG* 180: 21-24

Levi in his book *Biopneuma*, affirms the traditional day of
the Ascension as ten days before the Feast of Pentecost:
'After the Manifested light had returned to the glory of
the Eternal, ten days were spent by the Twelve in prepara-
tion ...' - *Biopneuma*, Pg. 52

Pentecost - Whitsunday - Day of Christine Power
'Now, when the day of Pentecost had come Jerusalem was
filled with pious Jews and proselytes from many lands.
The Christines all were met and were in perfect harmony.'
- *AG* 182: 1-2

'This is the day of Christine power; the day that he, the
man from Galilee, is glorified.' - *AG* 182: 19

Christmas - Dec. 25ᵗʰ - Feast of the Nativity of Jesus - 'At midnight came a cry, a child is born in yonder cave among the
beasts. And lo, the promised son of man was born.' - *AG*
3: 4

The Sabbath, The Day of Good Works & Prayer

Sabbath - All Saturdays devoted to prayer and serving
God through serving mankind.
'But Jesus said, Was man designed to fit the Sabbath, or
was the Sabbath day designed to fit the man?' - *AG* 74: 10

'Jesus said, My Father works on Sabbath days and may not I?

He sends his rain, his sunshine and his dew; he makes his grass to grow, his flowers to bloom; he speeds the harvests just the same on Sabbath days as on the other days.

If it is lawful for the grass to grow and flowers to bloom on Sabbath days it surely is not wrong to succour stricken men.' - *AG* 91: 25-27

'The Sabbath day was made for man; man was not made to fit the Sabbath day.

The man is son of God and under the eternal law of right, which is the highest law, he may annul the statute laws.' - *AG* 93: 9-10

'The number of the Holy Breath is seven, and God holds in his hands the sevens of time.

In forming worlds he rested on the seventh day, and every seventh day is set apart as Sabbath day for men. God said, The seventh is the Sabbath of the Lord thy God; remember it and keep it wholly set apart for works of holiness; that is, for works not for the selfish self, but for the universal self.

Men may do work for self upon the six days of the week; but on the Sabbath of the Lord they must do naught for self.

This day is consecrated unto God; but man serves God by serving man.' - *AG* 96: 23-27

The Memorials of Jesus & John

Good Friday - private fast & services optional; conse-crations & initiations appropriate - *AG* 165-171

Jesus said: 'The time will come when God will let you have your way, and you will do to me what Herod did to John; and in the awfulness of that sad hour these men will fast.' - *AG* 119: 27-28

'Now, on the day before the Sabbath day, the twelve disciples who had received the call were met with one ac-cord in Jesus' home.

And Jesus said to them, This is the day to consecrate yourselves unto the work of God; so let us pray.' - *AG* 89: 1-2

'Then Jesus said, The vital force of men depends on what they eat and drink. Is spirit-life the stronger when the vital force is weak? Is sainthood reached by starving, self imposed? A glutton is a sinner in the sight of God, and he is not a saint who makes himself a weakling and unfitted for the heavy tasks of life by scorning to make use of God's own means of strength.' - *AG* 119: 13-15

Decollation of John - Aug. 29th , the martyrdom of John the Harbinger (Baptist); decollation means beheading - *AG* 117. The Christines did not keep this fast. - *AG* 119

Other Scripturally Based Feasts

New Year's Day - Circumcision - Jan. 1ˢᵗ - Jesus' circumcised foreskin forming a circle represents time

Epiphany - Jan. 6ᵗʰ, the Baptism of Jesus, actually a more ancient feast than Christmas

Candlemas - Presentation in the Temple - Feb. 2ⁿᵈ, the coming of the wise men, martyrdoms of Zacharias and the Holy Innocents, though not kept as a fast

Annunciation - Mar. 25ᵗʰ - Gabriel announcing Jesus' birth - *AG* 2

Palm Sunday - Triumphal Entry into Jerusalem - AG 151

Holy Monday - Cleansing of the Temple - *AG* 152

Holy Tuesday - Glorification and Illumination of Jesus in the Temple - *AG* 153-157

Holy Wednesday - Anointing of Jesus by Mary - *AG* 158-159

Holy Saturday - Easter Vigil - Entombment of Jesus' physical body - *AG* 172

Low Saturday - Christophany (appearance of Jesus Resurrected) in the Temple - *AG* 177

Low Sunday - Thomas' Easter - Christophany unto Thomas - *AG* 177

Lammas - July 25ᵗʰ - Aug. 1ˢᵗ - Nativity of John, five months before Jesus' birth - *AG* 2

Transfiguration - Aug. 6ᵗʰ, Jesus transfigured beside the Ascended Masters Moses and Elijah - *AG* 129

Nativity of Mary - Sept. 8ᵗʰ - AG 1

All Hallows - Oct. 25ᵗʰ - Nov. 1ˢᵗ - Gabriel announcing John's birth - *AG* 2

The following verses are for use in both private devotion and services. It is adapted from the *AG*, some I AM Movement decrees, and other wonderful sources, specifically for ease in spoken word. Often selections are paraphrased, modernized and reworked for greater empowerment of the individual and for more lucid comprehension. The number at the end of a stanza is the chapter number that it was adapted from in the *AG*.

Christine Salutations of Peace

1. Peace, peace on earth, good will to men!

2. Peace be to all; good will to all!

3. Peace be to everyone of you, goodwill to all mankind.

Invocations

4. The Logos is the Perfect Word, [Jahhevahe]; that which creates; that which destroys and that which saves. 48

5. Say Jahhevahe. This do for seven times and you shall see. 138

6. In the name of the Father, the Mother and Christ the Son.

7. God the Father, the Power;
God the Mother, the Wisdom;
Christ the Son, the Love.

8. In the name of God the Father,
Jehovah, God of Power;
And God the Mother, Visel, Goddess of Wisdom;
And God the Son, Christ, God of Love.

9. Heavenly Father send us Thy blessings from up above,
Divine Mother shower us with Thy grace on the wings of a dove,
Lord Christ show us the Way to make manifest Thy Love.

10. Jahhevahe, O Being of Dazzling White Fire and Flame;
Jahhevahe, Word of Power, Omnific Word, O Sacred Name;
Jahhevahe, O Jewel of the Lotus, Thy Diamond Heart enfold us.

11. *The Three Great Manifestations of Christ*

Prince Oromasis, Lord Zarathustra, Lord Enoch
the Christ, the Initiate,
Adon Mashich Cumi, Lord Christ Arise!
Lord Maitreya, the Lord of Love, Lord Melchisedec
the Christ, Prince of Peace and King of Justice,
Adon Mashich Cumi, Lord Christ Arise!
Lord Jesus the Christ, Jehoshua Mashich, Immanuel,
Prince of Peace and King of Kings,
Adon Mashich Cumi, Lord Christ Arise!

12. *The Seven Mighty Elohim*

O Mighty Elohim Arcturus and Ahura Mazda,
Beloved Sanat Kumara, the Ancient of Days
O Mighty Elohim of Peace and the Dawn
O Mighty Elohim Cyclopea and the Great Silent
Watcher of the Earth
O Mighty Elohim of Purity and Mighty Astrea
O Mighty Elohim Orion and Beloved Sananda
O Mighty Elohim Cassiopeia and Helios, the Solar
Ruler
O Mighty Elohim Hercules and Surya, the Maitreya

13. *The Seven Holy Archangels & Virtues*

Lord Michael, Prince of Angels

Christine, Angel of Illumination and the Church
The Angel of Gethsemane, Angel of Love
Archangel Gabriel, Keeper of the Scrolls
Beloved Mary, mother of Jesus, Queen of Angels
Archangel Uriel, Messenger of Peace
Archangel Zadkiel, Angel of Mercy

The Archangelic Virtues

Faith, Hope, and Grace

14. *The Lord Michael Decree of Traveling Protection*

Lord Michael before, Lord Michael behind,
Lord Michael to the left, Lord Michael to the right,
Lord Michael above, Lord Michael below,
Lord Michael, Lord Michael, wherever I go.
I AM his Love protecting here,
I AM his Love protecting here,
I AM his Love protecting here.
- a basic decree of The Summit Lighthouse, Inc.

15. *The Ascended Aquarian Masters*

(Purple Ray): Lord Jesus the Christ,

(Pink Ray): Nada,
and John the Beloved

(White Ray): Elijah

(Aqua Ray): Moses
and Djwal Kul

(Blue Ray): The Divine Director,
Morya

(Violet Ray): and Saint Germain

(Yellow Ray): Kuthumi and Lanto

Chananda,
and Beloved Levi, Messenger of the Aquarian Age

16. Logos Circle Seven;
On earth as it is in Heaven!

Decrees, Prayers and Praise

17. *The Pillar of Light* I

a. O Mighty I AM Spirit bright,
Immerse me in thy Light.
I call forth now in God's Name,
Baptize me in the Violet Flame.

b. Let it keep my temple free

From all discord sent to me,
Every minute, every hour,
Love, Wisdom and Power!

c. I AM baptized in Violet Fire;
I AM the Purity of Divine Desire;
Every minute, every hour,
Love, Wisdom and Power!

d. I AM Light, Thou Christ in me
Setting us forever free,
Every minute, every hour,
Love, Wisdom and Power!

18. *The Pillar of Light* II
O Mighty Jahhevahe bright,
Enfold me in thy Pillar of Light.
In the Omnific Word, Thy Sacred Name,
Baptize me in the Violet Flame.

19. *The Pillar of Light* III

O Mighty I AM Spirit Divine,
Around me Thy Light doth shine,
I command now in Thy Name,
Baptize me in the Violet Flame.

20. *The Pillar of Light* IV

I AM in the Pillar of Light.
I AM baptized in Violet Fire;
I AM immersed in the Light
I AM the Purity of Divine desire.

21. *The Wall of Blue Flame of Protection*

O Mighty I AM Spirit Bright
Place around the Pillar of Light
The Wall of Violet-Blue Fire
Keep me free from all discordant desire.

22. Forgive men their trespasses and your Heavenly
Father will forgive you. - Biopneuma, Pg. 84

23. Father, forgive them for they know not what
they do.

24. I AM forgiving everyone everywhere;
And now, I AM forgiven completely, perfectly and
eternally.
I AM Free! I AM Free! I AM Free!

25. *The Perfect Prayer*

Our Father and Mother who art in Heaven;

Holy is Thy name. Thy Kingdom is come!
Thy will is being done!
Heaven and earth are one!
Give us today the Bread of Heaven.
We are forgiven,
As we have forgiven others.
Lead us unto the Eternal Victory of Salvation,
That we inherit through Thy Grace.
For thine is the Kingdom, the Power and the Glory,
Lord Christ, for ever and ever. Amen. 59

26. *The Model Prayer*

Our Father-God who art in Heaven;
Holy is Thy Name.
Thy Kingdom come;
Thy will be done on earth as it is in Heaven.
Give us this day our needed bread.
Help us to forget, each and every debt.
And shield us from the tempter's snare, That is hard
for us to bear;
Give us the strength to overcome.
For Thine is the Power and the Glory and the
Kingdom, forever and ever. Amen. 94; 137

27. a. I AM forgiveness expanding here,
Blasting out all doubt and fear,
Setting mankind forever free,

On Wings of Light and Victory.

b. I AM calling God the Power
For forgiveness every hour;
To every one in every place,
I AM expanding forgiving grace.

28. *I AM Affirmations of Jesus the Christ*

a. I AM come from God
I AM the Resurrection and the Life
I AM the Ascension in the Light

b. I AM the Vine
I AM the Bread of Heaven
I AM the Cup of Life

c. I AM the Door
I AM the Truth
I AM the Way

d. I AM Life
I AM Light
I AM Love

e. I AM come to help
I AM come to save the world
I AM with you always, even unto the end of the world.

29. a. O Mighty Elohim Cassiopea,
Crown me with Thy Golden Flame of Wisdom,
And illumine my soul,
Help me to become
Perfect, radiant and whole.

b. O Angel of Illumination, Mighty Christine,
I call unto thee in Our Mother's Holy Name.
Make my thoughts perfect and pristine
And send forth thy Angels of Golden Flame.

30. a. O Mighty Elohim Arcturus,
Blaze the Violet Flame through us!
Violet Fire of Mercy Divine,
Blaze within in this heart of mine!

b. Lord Zadkiel, Angel of Mercy
Send forth the Violet Flame Angels,
Transmute all discord with Violet Fire,
Make me a Being of Divine Desire!

31. a. O Mighty Elohim Hercules,
Lord Michael and Faith,
Protect me with thy Loving Power,
Every second, every minute, every hour.

b. Lord Michael, Lord Michael, I call unto thee
Dispel all discord and now set me free,

166

Wield Thy Flaming Sword of bright blue,
With Fiery Lightning of blue-white hue!

32. a. O Mighty Elohim Cyclopea,
Perfect my mind, body and feeling.
Thou Great Elohim of Healing,
Divine Scientist with Eye All-Seeing,
Fill with Light my very being.

b. I AM God's Perfection manifest
In mind, body and soul.
I AM God's Power flowing
To heal and keep me whole.

c. Beloved Mary, mother of Jesus,
Blaze forth the Healing Aqua Flame,
Every minute, every hour,
Love, Wisdom, and Power!

d. O atoms, cells and electrons
Within this body of mine,
Let God's Perfection
Make me now Divine!

33. a. O Elohim of Purity and Mighty Astrea,
Immerse me in thy Flame of White,
Archangel Gabriel and Hope,
Help me Ascend into the Light!

b. O Beloved Mighty Astraea
Wield Thy Flaming Sword of bright blue,
Dispel all discord with the Light so true,
And Fiery Lightning of blue-white hue!

34. a. O Mighty Elohim Orion,
Help me to be a minister of Love,
Expanding Divine Compassion
From Heaven above.

b. O Mighty Elohim Orion,
Send forth Fire and Flame of Lavender-pink,
Blaze it through me and guard
What I do, say and think.

c. O Angel of Gethsemane, Archangel of Love
Send forth thy Lavender Flame Angels
On Heavenly wings of Light Divine;
Blaze the Flame of Love through this heart of mine.

35. a. O Mighty Elohim of Peace,
Bestow upon us thy Grace;
Send forth Divine Tranquility
Through time and space!

b. O Mighty Elohim of Peace,
Archangel Uriel and Grace,
Send forth the Purple Flame of Tranquility

To all life in every place.

36. *The Return to Eden*

I AM in a New Heaven on earth.
I AM in a New Garden of Eden.
I AM in the Eternal Paradise.
I AM in the Father's Kingdom.
I AM, I AM, I AM! World without end!

37. Prepare, O prepare; the Prince of Peace shall come, and now is coming on the clouds of Heaven. 57

38. All Strength, All Wisdom and All Love be yours, Immanuel. 3

39. Jesus is the Christ; the King who was to come, praise God!

40. Most blessed be the name of God, for He has opened up the Fount of Blessings.
Behold, for soon the Day Star from on high will come, to light the Way for those who sit within the darkness, and guide our ways to the feet of Peace. 2

41. *The Song of Mary and Salome*

Today I AM in exultation great;
My thoughts and all Life seem lifted up.
This is a day of exultation;
A day of worship and of praise;
A day when, in a measure, we may comprehend Our
Father-God. 9

42. *The Song of Salome*

Behold the sun! It manifests the Power of God who
speaks to us through sun, moon and stars, through
mountain, hill and vale;
Through flower, plant and tree.
God sings for us through birdsong, harpsichord
and human voice;
He speaks to each heart; and each heart must speak
to him; and this is prayer.
Prayer is the ardent wish that every way of
Life be Light; that every act be crowned with Good;
that every living thing be prospered by our ministry.
A noble deed, a helpful word is prayer.
The fount of prayer is in the heart;
by thought, not words, the heart is carried up to
God, where it is blest, then let us pray.
[Several minutes of silent prayer]
The blessings of the Three and of the Seven, Who
stand before the throne, will surely rest upon you
evermore. 12

43. *The Book of Life Prayer*

We thank Thee Father, the Lord of Heaven and earth, because Thou hast revealed Thyself to babes, and taught them how to light the Path and lead the wise to Thee.

What Thou hast given to Jesus the Christ, lo, he hast given to us, and through the Sacred Word [Jahhevahe], he hast bestowed on us the understanding heart.

That we may know and honor Thee through Christ, who was, and is, and evermore shall be. 14

44. *At the Resurrection of Lazarus*

My Father-God, Thou hast ever heard my prayers, I thank Thee.

I AM Thine and Thou art mine, make strong the Word of Power [Jahhevahe]. 148

45. Prayer of the Troubled Soul

My Father-God, I would not ask to be relieved of all the burdens I must bear;

I only ask for grace and strength to bear the burdens whatever they may be.

O Father, I glorify Thy name! 156

46. *Song of Victory - a Song of Miriam*

Bring forth the harp, bring forth the cymbal, all ye
choirs of Heaven,
Join in the song, the new, new song.
The Lord, with His own Hand has pulled back the
curtains of the night;
The sun of Truth is flooding Heaven and earth;
God is our strength and our song;
Our salvation and our hope, and we will build a
New House for Him;
We will cleanse and purify our hearts.
We are the Temple of the Holy Breath.
We are the Tabernacle of God;
We are the Holy Land;
We are the New Jerusalem;
Allelujah, praise the Lord! 110

47. *The Day Star - a Song of Miriam*
All Hail the Day Star from on high!
All hail the Christ who was, is and evermore shall
be!
All hail the dawn of peace on earth; good will to
men!
All hail Triumphant King, who brings to Light
Immortal Life for men!
All hail the Triumph of the soul!
All hail the empty tomb!
All hail! For he has called the pure in heart to sit
with Him upon the throne of Power!

All hail the rending veil!
The Way unto God is open for mankind!
Bring forth the harp and touch its highest strings;
Bring forth the lute, and sound its sweetest notes!
For the low, are high exalted now, and they who walked in darkness and in the vale of death, are risen up and God and man are one for evermore, Allelujah! Praise the Lord for evermore. Amen. 146

Purification - The Fount of Wisdom

48. The cleansing of the soul is by Purity in Life. The Kingdom of the Soul, is not of outward show, but is the Church Within. 15

49. The Silence is where the soul meets God, and there the Fount of Wisdom is;
All who enter are immersed in Light, and filled with Wisdom, Love and Power. 40

50. The Silence is the Kingdom of the Soul, not seen by human eyes.
If you would find this Silence of the Soul you must prepare the Way.
None but the pure in heart may enter here.
You must lay aside all tenseness in the mind, all business cares, all fears, all doubts and troubled thoughts.

Your human will must be absorbed by the Divine; then you will come into a Consciousness of Holiness.

Within the Holy Place you will see upon a Living Shrine the Candle of the Lord aflame.

And when you see It blazing there, look deep within the Temple of your brain, and you will see It all aglow.

Throughout the Temple of the body are candles waiting to be lighted by the flaming torch of Love.

And when you see the candles all aflame, just look, and you will see, with eyes of soul, the Waters of the Fount of Wisdom rushing on; and you may drink freely.

Behold there, the hidden Bread of Life; and he who eats shall never die. 40

51. Faith is the healing water of every drop of water of this spring.

He who believes with all his heart that he will be made whole by washing in this fount will be made whole when he has washed; and he may wash at any time. 41

52. *The Fount of Life*

The Fount of Life is not a little pool;
it is as wide as the spaces of the heavens.

The waters of the fount are Love; and he who plunges deep into the Living Springs, in Living Faith, may wash away his guilt and be made whole, and freed from sin. 41

53. *John speaks on Christ*

In water I do cleanse, symbolic of the cleansing of the soul; but when Christ comes, he will cleanse in Holy Breath and purify in fire. 63

54. *Born Again*

Except a man be born again he cannot see the King; he cannot comprehend the words I speak.
The birth of which I speak is not the birth of flesh.
Except a man be born of the Holy Breath, he cannot come into the Kingdom of the Holy One.
That which is born of flesh is child of man; That which is born of Holy Breath is child of God.

55. *The Christine Gate*

You men of every nation, hear!
Come unto me, the Christine Gate is opened up, turn from your sins and enter through the gate and see the King.
Enter through the Christine Gate into the Kingdom

of the Holy One! 78

56. *Words of John*

In water I have washed the people who have turned
from sin, symbolic of the cleansing of the soul;
But Jesus bathes forever in the Living Waters of the
Holy Breath. 79

57. This is the day to consecrate ourselves unto the
work of God; so let us pray.
Turn from the outer to the inner self.
And you will be baptized in Holy Breath.

58. *Humility*

There is no honored seat at Heaven's Feast except
for him who humbly takes the lowest seat.
May these feet walk in the ways of Righteousness
for evermore.
The feet are truly symbols of the understanding of
man, and he who would be clean must, in the Living
Stream of Life, wash well his understanding everyday. 160

Communion - *The Feast of Life*

59. God feeds the soul direct from Heaven, the

Bread of Life comes from above.

60. My Father-God is King of all mankind, and He has sent me forth with all the bounties of his matchless Love and boundless wealth. To all people of all lands, I bear these gifts; this Water and Bread of Life. And we will meet again, for in my Fatherland is room for all, I will prepare a place for you. 36

61. *Jacob's Well*

Know the blessings that Our Father-God has sent to us through Christ!
He will gladly give you a cup of water from the Fount of Life, and you will never thirst again.
The water flows from springs that never fail.
For when we drink the water, we become a well, and from inside ourselves the sparkling waters bubble up into Eternal Life. 81

62. Behold, the Feast of Life is spread for you; come in faith and take the Bread of Life. 102

63. I find myself at rest within the arms of God, whose blessed messengers bring down to me the Bread of Life. 105

64. Seek not for food that perishes, but seek for

food that feeds the soul; and lo, I bring you food from Heaven.

Lo, the Christ has come; He is the Bread of Life that God has given the world.

And they who eat this Bread of Heaven, and drink these Waters from the Spring of Life cannot be lost; they feed the soul, and purify the Life.

Behold, for God has said, When man has purified himself I will exalt him to the throne of Power. 125

65. *The Keys of Heaven*

The Christ is Everlasting Life;
He came from Heaven;
He has the keys of Heaven, and no man enters except he fills himself with Christ.

66. There is no one who can pronounce the Sacred Word, [Jahhevahe] and in the name of Christ restore the sick, and cast out unclean spirits, who is not a child of God.

Whoever gathers in the Grain of Heaven is one with us. Whoever gives a cup of water in the name of Christ is one with us; so God will judge. 131

67. Whoever is athirst may come to Christ and drink. He who believes in Jesus and in the Christ whom God has sent, may drink the Cup of Life, and from

inside himself shall streams of Living Waters flow. The Holy Breath will overshadow him, and he will breathe the Breath, and speak the Word, [Jahhevahe] and live the Life. 134

68. Jesus said, Lo, I have gone before you many moons, and I have given you the Bread of Heaven and the Cup of Life. 140

69. The Lord of Heaven and earth has spread a sumptuous feast, and you were bidden first of all; The many have been called, but chosen are the few. 153

70. *I AM the Feast of Life*

I AM the Bread of Heaven
I AM the Bread of Life
I AM the Living Bread which comes from Heaven.
I AM the Body of Christ

I AM the Cup of Life
I AM the Cup of Blessing
I AM a Fountain of Living Waters
I AM the Blood of Christ

Marriage

71. And Jesus said, There is no tie more sacred than the marriage tie.

The chain that binds two souls in Love is made in Heaven, and man can never sever it in twain. 70

72. Love is the Power of God that binds two souls and makes them one;

There is no power on earth that can dissolve the bond.

The bodies may be forced apart by man or death for just a little time; but they will meet again. 98

73. God made a woman for a man, and they were one; and afterwards he said,

A man shall leave his father and his mother and shall cleave unto his wife; they are no more divided, they are one, one flesh. What God has joined no man can part. 143

Consecration

74. *Hearts of Purity and Love*

Only the Holy Breath can fan your fires into a Living Flame and make them Light.

And Holy Breath can raise the ethers of the fires to

Light in none but hearts of Purity and Love.

Make pure the heart, admit the Holy Breath, and then you will be full of Light.

And like a city on a hill, your Light will shine afar and light the Way for others. 107

75. *The Omnific Word*

Receive the Holy Breath.

I give you the Word of Power [Jahhevahe].

By this Omnific Word you shall cast spirits out, shall heal the sick and bring the dead to Life again.

As you go proclaim, The Kingdom of Christ has come! 122;123

76. Receive ye the Holy Breath.

This breath of true Inspiration brings one into the higher ethers

where the River of Life flows unsullied from the Dive Throne,

where the Trees of Immortal Life grow in their beauty;

where the Fountain of Wisdom flows on forever

and where the Sun of Righteousness floods all the plains with the Light of Health and deathlessness. - Levi, SC, Pp. 56-57

77. The Light will come and then you will know that
I AM the I AM. 135

78. I AM the Lamp;
Christ is the Oil of Life;
The Holy Breath the Fire.
Behold the Light!
Walk in the Light of Life! 135

79. I AM the Candle of the Lord aflame to light
the Way; and while you have the Light walk in the
Light. 72

Healing

80. *Perfect Health*
I will be in perfect health;
I will be able to heal others;
The Holy Spirit will be my helper.

I AM in perfect health;
I AM able to heal others;
The Mother God is my helper. - Biopneuma, Pg. 71

81. When one has faith in God, in nature and one-
self; and knows the Word of Power,
[Jahhevahe]; the Word is cure for all the ills of
Life. The healer is one who can inspire faith. 23

82. The virtue from the hand or breath may heal a thousand; but Love is queen.
Love, is God's great healing balm. 23

83. My Father-God, let Power Divine overshadow me, and let the Holy Breath fill full your child and servant. 36

84. The very air we breathe is filled with balm of Life. Breathe in this balm of Life in faith and be whole. 41

85. *The Lily and the Rose*

The greatest Power in Heaven and earth is Thought. God made the universe by Thought; he paints the lily and the rose with Thought. Why think it strange that I should send a healing Thought and change the ethers of disease and death to those of health and Life?
Lo, you shall see far greater things than this, for by the Power of Holy Thought, my body will be changed from carnal flesh to Spirit Form, and so will yours! 84

86. *The Keys to Life and Death*

By the Omnific Word [Jahhevahe], you may control

the elements, and all the powers of the air. And when within your souls you speak this Word, you have the keys to Life and death; of things that are; of things that were; of things that are to be.

87. Lord Jesus, if you speak the Word, [Jahhevahe], I know thy servant will be well. 102

Eternal Life

88. *Jesus Resurrecting*

All hail the rising sun, the coming of the day of righteousness! 172

89. The Resurrected Jesus the Christ
I conquered death and arose; brought Immortality to Light and painted on the wall of time a rainbow for the sons of men; what I did all men shall do; and what I AM all men will be. 176

90. It is not well to weep because of death.
Death is no enemy to man; it is a friend who, when the work of life is done, just cuts the cord that binds the human heart to earth, that it may sail on smoother seas.

91. Jesus said, Weep not, I AM the Life. 102

92. The Resurrected Jesus the Christ
He lifted up his hands and said, I AM.
Then the disciples knew it was the Lord.
And Jesus said, Behold for human flesh can be
transmuted into higher form, and then that higher
form is master of things manifest, and can at will,
take any form. 173

93. I AM your Lord, and I have risen from the dead.
I often said, I will arise. 175

94. *The Crown of Light*

Jesus came and sat with them; a Crown of Light was
on his head.
And Jesus said, My brothers of the Silent
Brotherhood, peace, peace on earth; goodwill to
men! A son of man has risen from the dead. This
flesh in which I come to you was changed with
speed of Light from human flesh into Flesh Divine.
And so I AM come, the first of all the race to be
transmuted to the image of the I AM. What I have
done, all men will do;
And what I AM, all men will be! 176

95. All hail! For I AM risen from the dead, first
fruitage of the grave! 175

96. I came to earth to demonstrate the resurrection fo the dead, the transmutation of the carnal man to Flesh of Man Divine.177

97. Behold, for I have risen from the dead with gifts for men. I give you all Power in Heaven and earth. Go and teach the nations of earth the Gospel of the Resurrection of the dead and Eternal Life through Christ, the Love of God. What I can do all men can do. 178

98. I AM the Resurrection and the Life. The dead shall live and many that shall live will never die. Christ will lift the sons and daughters of the human race, from darkness and graves, to Light and Everlasting Life.
I AM the manifest of Love raised from the dead. 178

99. We will be quickened by the Holy Breath, will raise the substance of the body to a higher tone, and make it like the substance of the bodies of the planes above.
Life springs from death; the carnal form is changed to Form Divine.
The will of man makes possible the action of the Holy Breath.
When the will of man and the Will of God are One,

the Resurrection is a fact.
This is the chemistry of mortal life, the ministry of death, the Mystery of Deific Life. What I have done all men can do, and what
I AM all men shall be. 178

Inspiration and Illumination

100. Behold, I came a Light unto the world; he who believes in me shall walk in Light, the Light of Life. 156

101. Our God is Spirit, and in Him all Wisdom, Love and Strength abide. 84

102. Our God is Spirit; they who worship Him must worship Him in Spirit and in truth. 81

103. God is Spirit, and in Spirit men must worship if they would attain a Consciousness of God. 96

104. The Good shine forth as suns in the Kingdom of the Soul. 116

105. Every thought and wish is photographed and then preserved within the Book of Life to be revealed at any time the masters will. 109

106. The perfect age will not require forms and rites. The perfect age will come when everyone will be a priest (minister). 35

107. Behold the Kingdom of the Christ! It is as old as God, and yet it is as new as morning sun; it contains only the truth. 120

108. Lo, you have solved a mystery; you are within the Kingdom and the Kingdom is within you.
The Kingdom of Heaven is within. 155

109. *The Pearl of Great Price*

Take up your cross and follow me through Christ into the path of true discipleship; the path that leads to Life. This Way of Life is called the pearl of great price, and he who finds it must put all he has beneath his feet. 142

110. *The Transfiguration*

As he prayed a brilliant light appeared; his form became as radiant as precious stone; his face shone like the sun; his garments seemed as white as snow; the son of man became the Son of God.
He was transfigured that the men of earth might see the possibilities of man. 129

111. *The Transfiguration*

Heaven and earth are one; masters there and masters here are one. The veil that separates the worlds is but an ether veil. For those who purify their hearts by faith the veil is rolled aside, and they can see and know that death is an illusive thing. 129

112. *The Ascension*

All Power in Heaven and earth is given unto me, and now I bid you go to all the world and preach the Gospel of the Christ, the unity of God and man, the Resurrection of the dead, and of Eternal Life. And now I will ascend to God, as you and all the world will rise to God. 180

113. *Whitsunday - Pentecost*

This is the day of Christine Power; the day that he, the man from Galilee is glorified.
This day the Christine Church is opened up, and whosoever will may enter in, and by the boundless grace of Christ, be saved. 182

114. Attended by a retinue of couriers of the angel world, he ascended to the throne of God.
And now being exalted high and full of Holy Breath,

he breathes on us again. 182

115. The time will come when all Life will be evolved
unto the State of Perfection.
And after man is Man in Perfectness, he will evolve
to higher forms of Life. 32

116. The great work of masters is to restore the
heritage of man;
to return him to his estate he lost,
when he will live again upon the ethers of his native
plane. 32

117. Heaven is not far away; it is not a place to be
reached; it is a state of mind.
Now, cease to seek for Heaven in the sky;
just open up your hearts, and like a flood of Light,
Heaven will come and bring a boundless joy. 33

118. The Kingdom of the Holy One is the Bride;
and Christ is the Groom. 79

119. Christ is the King of Righteousness;
Christ is the Love of God; He is God;
One of the Holy Persons of the Triune God.
Christ lives in every heart of Purity.
Jesus comes to bring the Savior of the world to
men; Love is the Savior of the world. 79

120. The blessings of the Three and of the Seven, who stand before the throne, will surely rest upon you evermore. 12

121. Your sins are all forgiven; your faith has saved you; go in peace. 104

122. Our Father-God, let now Thy servants go in peace, for we have seen the glory of the Lord. 47

123. The benedictions of the Christ abide with you for evermore. 140

124. My Father-God, let now the benedictions of Thy Love, Thy mercy and Thy truth rest upon us. 146

125. *The Benediction at the Ascension*

The benedictions of the Holy Ones, of the Almighty God, and of the Holy Breath, of Christ the Love of God made manifest, will rest upon you always. 180

Glossary

Adam Kadmon - "Father Time"; "Primal Man." The Adi-Manu, the primordial Manu of the Spirit Realm. See Manu.

Adi-Buddha - The primordial Buddha, Sanat Kumara. See Ahura Mazda; Ormazd; Sanat Kumara.

Adi-Manu - The primordial Manu of the Spirit Realm, also known as Adam Kadmon. See Manu

Adon Mashich Cumi - (ah - dohn - mah - sheek - koo - mee) "Lord Christ Arise!" The words used at the Resurrection of Jesus the Christ by the Masters of the Silent Brotherhood.

Ahura Mazda - (ah - who - ruh - Mazda) "wise Lord." Zoroastrian (Avestan) name for the Elohim Arcturus; later the name evolved into Ormazd in later Persian, Oromasdes (Oromasis) by the Greeks. See Sanat Kumara.

Akasha - (uh - cash - uh). Sanskrit term meaning ether; the etheric plane where the highest spiritual planes, the Throne of God, and Heaven are located; our original home. Akasha which is within us, has proceeded to expand in the Realm or Plane of Soul and will continue to expand into this physical plane which will transform this world into Heaven on Earth.

Akashic Records - The Book of Life, the Rolls of Graphael; a supernatural, Divine, living super-computer which records every thought and action in the universe. Every thought and action leaves an etheric imprint which is recorded, upon our return to the Realm of Soul, our entire life is viewed and reviewed on a giant screen. Anyone who has had their 'life flash before them' has experienced it. Levi Dowling was able to perfectly review and playback the entire life of Jesus and transcribe *The AG*. Technological advances divinely inspired by the Akashic Records are computers, television, plasma television, digital cameras/television, the Internet, etc. See Graphael; Rolls of Graphael.

Apollo - "son of light." (1) Another name of the Elohim Cassiopeia. See Cassiopeia; Mithra. (2) The Grecian Master, Defender of the Oracle of Delphi, one of the Seven Sages; The Maha Chohan. See Apollonius of Tyana; Maha Chohan.

Apollonius of Tyana - (apple - loh - knee - us - uhv - tie- uh - nuh); Apollonius meaning "father lion"; "father light." Pythagorean philosopher and miracle worker, said to have journeyed to Persia and India to study with the Magi; studied in the Temple of Jagganath; ascended in front of his followers. He was considered the incarnation of Apollo (Cassiopeia.) He is known as Apollo, the Grecian Master, the Defender of the Oracle (of Delphi) and one of the Seven Sages in *The AG*. See Maha Chohan.

Aqua - A sacred color; associated with Emerald Green, a bluish green and the highest (fastest) vibration of green ascending towards blue; a color representing water, foliage, life, Akasha, crystal(s), healing, supply and the Elohim Cyclopea; the Aqua Flame and Light confers healing, inspiration, supply, and science.

Aquaria - (1) Another name for Quan Yin, the Seraphim of Aquarius (Water-bearer); s'Akmaquil, who in The Cusp of the Ages in the *AG* is the co-ruler of the Age of Aquarius, the Spiritual Age. (2) Esoterically, another name for Visel, the Mother God; thus, the Aquarian Age, the Spiritual Age, the Age of the Mother. [40]

Aquarian - (1) Referring to the Age of Aquarius; the Golden Age; the Spiritual Age; the Age of the Holy Spirit, the Mother God; the Age of the Return of Christ, hence the title "The Aquarian Gospel of Jesus the Christ of the Piscean Age" [official title]. (2) Aquarian Christine, Christine.

Astrochristology - "study of the stars through Christ." The Sacred Christine astrology of invocation, blessing and symbolism; unconnected to Babylonian horoscopes associated with vulgar or popular astrology, which is unscientific fortune telling and full of negative influences, suggestions and ideas.

Baptism by Blood - Martyrdom. Jesus the Christ said: 'The self and greed and doubt will rage into a fever heat, and then, because of me, the earth will be baptized in human blood.' - AG 117: 13

Baptism by Fire - The visualization, meditation and feeling of being immersed in the flames of the Sacred Fire. See Immersion in Light.

Baptism by the Holy Breath (Spirit) - Sanctification by the Holy Spirit. The Holy Breath fans the flame of the Baptism by Fire. See Fire Baptism; Immersion in Light.

Baptism by Water - Rite symbolic of the cleansing of the soul instituted by John the Baptist in the Christian dispensation.

Blue - Sacred color; Blue fire and flame confer power

and protection to be encircled around the outside of the Tube of Light (Pillar of Light); Swords and crosses of blue fire and flame placed before and around oneself repels all negative influences.

Brahm - "prayer." God as an impersonal pervading force from which all aspects and manifests of Deity and the Universe emerged; Universal Spirit (Breath); Tao; I AM.

Buddha - "enlightened one"; "awakened one." Term applied to Gautama, but is used also to refer to the goal of every human. Jesus was a Buddha and everyone is a potential Buddha. See Adi-Buddha; Maitreya.

Christ - "anointed." Term referring to the Third Person the Trinity, God the Son; equated meanings are Life, Logos [the Word], Love. When one accepts Christ they become 'anointed' - Christine. To anoint someone with oil, blow air on them to bestow the Holy Breath and lay hands on them is referred to as "christing" someone. Everyone is a potential Christ, Jesus paved the Way to show us how we may achieve this. Many others have achieved this and every Age [2,000 year period] the Spirit of Christ comes in human form on this physical plane, but now the Christ is manifesting in every believer in Christ and are becoming Christ-bearers or Christines, this is one Aspect of the Second Coming, the other is the Return of Jesus in a visible and tangible way to all on this plane of existence . Every world, planet and star is sent a Christ, a manifestation of Divine Love, this is the Way of the Universe. See Buddha, Krishna; Maitreya; Melchisedec; Oromasis; Zoroaster.

Christine - "Christ-bearer." (1) The Bride of Christ; the Universal Church. (2) Sincere believer in Christ, especially an Aquarian Christine. (3) Feminine aspect of Archangel Cassiel (Jophiel); angelic patroness of the Aquarian Christine Church; The Christine Angel. (4) Angels of the Golden Flame of Illumination that protect and inspire Aquarian Christines; The Christine Angels. (5) A state of consciousness.

Demigods - The Four and Twenty elders, the Cherubim and Seraphim are referred to as the Demigods in *AG* 178: 23.

Divine Director - Spiritual teacher of Joseph (Saint Germain) and Jesus; known as Vidyapati in the *AG*, he appeared unto Jesus in the Ascended State to instruct him in the needs of the Piscean Age, the Christian dispensation and foretold of the needs of the Aquarian Age; he is the Manu or progenitor of the human race, who oversees all human embodiments. See Manu.

Djwal Kul - (jew - all - cool) "cool flame." Ascended Master who was embodied as Kaspar, one of the Magi and one of the Seven Sages in the AG; Ascended Master Djwal Kul is the bearer of the Aqua Flame of healing and supply.

Elijah (ell - lye - juh) "God the Lord"; "the strong Lord"; "whose God is Jehovah." The Hebrew prophet, an ascended being, an earlier embodiment of John the Harbinger (John the Baptist); the Manifest of Purity; the Ascended Master Elijah.

Elohim - (ell - loh - him) "mighty ones"; "shining ones." Seven Divine Spirits that stand before the throne of the Trinity, are incorporated into and are Aspects of God.; known also as the Lesser Gods and the Septonate.

Father God - Our Father, a person of the Trinity; Jehovah; referred to as Zeus, Thoth, and Parabrahm in different religions.

Feast of Life, Remembrance - Communion, Lord's Supper, Eucharist, or Mass of the Christian Dispensation. See Inner Light.

Fire Baptism - (1) Anointing and Laying on of Hands. (2) Meditation involving visualizing and feeling the Violet Flame and other flames associated with the Sacred Fire of God. (3) Religious experience where this occurs. See Baptism by Fire; Sevenfold Flame; Violet Flame.

Goddess of Wisdom - See Holy Breath, Mother God, Visel.

Gold - A sacred color which represents the Love that is Christ; the Gold Ray bestows Peace and Tranquility; the Golden Flame is the Illumination and Wisdom of God. See Sevenfold Flame.

Graphael - "might of God." The Recording Angel; Keeper of the Scrolls; Keeper of the Book of Life, the Akashic Records; another name for Archangel Gabriel. See Rolls of Graphael; Akashic Records.

Great White Brotherhood - a college of ascended Masters; identical to the Silent Brotherhood; the Ascended Host. See Silent Brotherhood.

Green - A somewhat sacred color that represents Life and Growth; concerning sacredness it should always be an emerald or bluish green; green must ascend in vibration into the aqua; murky and yellowish greens are considered negative. See Aqua.

Heaven - (1) The highest plane, the Realm of Spirit, our original home, Akasha. The Kingdom of Heaven is within and around us just not readily perceivable on this realm or plane of existence. See Realms. (2) A state of mind on any plane or realm.

Hell - (1) The physical plane on which we are currently living. See Realms. (2) A state of mind.

Hierarch - A priestly ruler. The title is given to Ascended Masters who rule one of the Seven Rays or an Age (2,000 year period.)

Hierophant - Priestly director of initiations who reveals mysteries unto the candidate.

Holy Breath - Holy Spirit, the Mother-God, a person of the Trinity, Visel, the Goddess Wisdom.

Holy Spirit - The Holy Breath; The Mother God. See Holy Breath, Mother God; Visel.

I AM - Brahm; the Word; Divine Spirit; God; Jahhevahe; Tao, I AM that I AM.

I AM Movement - religious movement with many similarities in teachings: Ascended Masters of the Great White Brotherhood; the Seven Mighty Elohim and the I AM Presence; The I AM Movement is responsible for: bringing the teachings of Saint Germain regarding the Violet Flame used in meditation and visualization. See I AM; I AM Spirit; Saint Germain; Violet Flame.

I AM Spirit- the individualized Aspect of God of each person, the individual's "angel" or "guardian angel," that part of us that is divine, our Divine and Real Self, one's Immortal and Perfect Spirit; the Mighty I AM Presence.

See Brahm; Tao.

Immersion in Light - Baptism in Light; being inclosed in the Pillar of Light, which is a bright white Light vibrating an almost bluish color.

'And Jesus said, There is a Silence where the soul may meet its God, and there the fount of wisdom is, and all who enter are immersed in light, and filled with wisdom, love and power.' - *AG* 40: 3

Inner Circle - The closest Apostles to Jesus who had greater Spiritual understanding and witnessed the Transfiguration of Jesus with Elijah and Moses; they were John the Beloved, his brother James and Peter; only John the Beloved ascended in that lifetime.

Inner Light - Quaker term referring to believers who do not observe rites and rituals like Baptism and Communion (Lord's Supper, Feast of Life), because they celebrate the rites in an inner and spiritual way. Christian Scientists and the Salvation Army also do not usually have outward rites or rituals. This is a Christine belief, although we may observe rites if desired, each individual may decide for themselves how they want to experience them.

'All forms and rites are symbols of the things that men must do within the temple of the soul.'

'The perfect age will not require forms and rites and carnal sacrifice. The coming age is not the perfect age, and men will call for object lessons and symbolic rites.' - *AG* 35

'Jesus told the twelve about the inner light that cannot fail; about the kingdom of the Christ within the soul; about the power of faith; about the secret of the resurrection of the dead; about immortal life, and how the living may go forth and help the dead.' - *AG* 128: 16-17

Jagganath - (jah - guh - not) "Lord of the World or the Universe" - A title of Krishna, the Maitreya; Jesus lived in the Temple of Jagganath in India where he studied Brahmanic law. See Krishna; Maitreya.

Jahhevahe - "I AM that I AM." The Sacred Name of God, the Word, the Logos, the Omnific Word, the substitute is Jehovah; it is used as a mantra in The Aquarian Christine Church. See I AM; Logos; Jehovah; Father God.

Jehoshua - (yay - hoe - shoe - uh) - Variant of Jesus or Joshua.

Jehovah - "I AM that I AM." The Father God; Parabrahm; Zeus.

John the Harbinger - "Jehovah is gracious." John the Baptist; Manifest of Purity; Ascended Master Elijah. See Elijah.

Krishna - "deep blue"; "all-attractive one." See Christ; Jagganath; Melchisedec; Maitreya.

Kuthumi - (the original compiler of The Vedas). Zara, one of the chief Magi in the *AG*; Ascended Master Kuthumi; he also embodied as Pythagorus and Saint Francis of Assisi.

Lanto - "Heaven"; "great orchid." Referring to Lao Tan (Lao Tzu) the teacher of Confucius, the Duke of Chou; Ascended Master Lanto, who embodied as Meng-Ste, the eldest of the Seven Sages. See Lao Tan.

Lao Tan (Lao Tzu) - "the old or venerable master" - founder of Taoism, the writer of the *Tao Te Ching* is Lao Tzu identified with Lao Tan, the Duke of Chou, scribe of the Chou Dynasty and teacher of traditional ritual to Confucius. See Lanto, Mencius.

Lavender - A sacred color that is the ascent of the color soft pink rising into the higher vibration of purple and violet; the Lavender Flame is the synthesis of soft pink representing love, purple representing grace and peace and violet represent grace and mercy; the Lavender Flame is an aspect of the Violet Flame, which transmutes all karma and negativity. See Pink, Purple, Violet.

Levi - "united." The Messenger of the Aquarian Age

who transcribed the *AG* from the Akashic Records; Levi Dowling; the Ascended Master Levi.

Limbo - (1) The astral plane, a lower plane closely associated with the current physical plane, the plane within the atmosphere where ghosts, demons, and many elemental spirits reside who are unable or do not desire to rise to higher planes of existence. (2) a state of mind. See Realms.

Logos - The Word, Christ. See Jahhevahe.

Logos Circle Seven - Jesus' secret name as an initiate in the Secret Brotherhood of the Great Lodge of Heaven and Earth. - *AG* 48

Lord - (1) God; God the Father; Jesus; the Holy Spirit; the usage in the Christian dispensation. (2) Title given to certain Manifests the Christ, such as: Lord Jesus; Lord Maitreya, and his two Aspects, Lord Krishna and Lord Buddha; and Lord Zarathustra. (3) Title given to Apollo, the Maha Chohan. (4) Title given to Archangel Michael as the Prince of Angels and Captain of the Lord's Host.

Lower Self - The inclination to be selfish, to do evil, to harm oneself, to abuse one's body; the devil or satan.

Magdala - "tower." Town or castle keep owned by Mary Magdalene where Jesus introduced the Christines to the

Miriam Nada. See Mary Magdalene, Miriam Nada.

Magi - The word 'magic' derives from 'magi'; wise priest-kings of Zoroastrianism; three were sent to bearing gifts by chief Magi to the infant Jesus, known as the Three Wise Men; the chief Magi were: Kaspar (Djwal Kul) who was the leader, Melzone (Morya) and Zara (Kuthumi); all three were members of the Silent Brotherhood (the Great White Brotherhood); Kaspar was also one of the Seven Sages; when Jesus met with the three chief Magi and the Three Wise Men, they formed a "Septonate" of Magi, therefore Jesus may be referred to as the Seventh Magi. See Djwal Kul; Kuthumi; Morya.

Maha Chohan - "great Lord or Spirit." Cherubim who manifested as Apollo (Apollonius of Tyana) and Homer; s'Agham, the Cherubim of Leo; an Aspect of Cassiopeia; representative of the Mother God, Holy Breath (Spirit); the Maha Chohan. See Apollo; Apollonius of Tyana.

Manetho - "gift of Thoth." Egyptian historian and Hierophant of the Temple of Heliopolis; a manifest of the Ascended Master Serapis.

Manifest of Christ - there are seven Manifests of Christ, who are three Great Beings, that are known: Lord Krishna (Maitreya); Seth the Anointed (Jesus); Enoch the Initiate (Prince Oromasis); Melchisedec the Christ

(Maitreya); Lord Zarathustra (Prince Oromasis); Lord Buddha (Maitreya); and Lord Jesus the Christ.

Manifest of Purity - Title bestowed on the Ascended Master Elijah, as being the Manifest of the Elohim of Purity when embodied as John the Harbinger.

Maitreya - "Lord of Love" - Esoteric name for the Cherubic Aspects of Surya, the Elohim of Sirius; they are all Aspects of Hercules or Hare Krishna; Krishna as the Future Buddha; Melchisedec; the Maitreya Buddha; Melchisedec the Christ; Lord Maitreya; Lord Melchisedec; Lord Krishna; Gautama Buddha.

Manu - "thinker"; "man." (1) A progenitor of humanity like Adam or Noah, who oversees human embodiment. (2) Name of the Hindu Noah and first man. See Divine Director.

Mary Magdalene - Owner of the castle keep of Magdala, an older wealthy woman and Christine disciple who donated goods, money and the use of her mansion for the Christines to congregate; she had been cured of "seven spirits of the air" who obsessed her; no where is it ever written in any scripture that Mary Magdalene was a prostitute; she has been confounded (confused) with the Miriam Nada who was introduced to the Christines by Jesus in a public assembly at Magdala and sang inspirational songs;

Mary Magdalene is often associated with the "Miriam" in Gnostic scriptures and the Nag Hammadi scrolls, who is actually the Miriam Nada; Mary Magdalene was the third person to witness the Resurrection of Jesus. See Nada.

Melchisedec - (mel - kizz - uh - deck) "king of justice." High Priest and King of Salem, later called Jerusalem, an manifest of the Maitreya; Melchisedec the Christ; Lord Maitreya; Lord Krishna; the Maitreya. See Maitreya.

Mencius - "visionary or bright master." The Ascended Master Lanto, who embodied as Mencius, the Second Sage Duke of Chou; Meng-Ste an Ascended Being who appeared unto Jesus and was one of the Seven Sages. See Lanto.

Mithra (Mithras, Mitra) - "friend"; "oath"; "sun." Name of the Elohim Cassiopeia, known anciently also as Apollo; Mithra is his name in Zoroastrianism; Mithras in the Mithraic Mysteries; and Mitra in Hinduism. See Apollo.

Morya - The Ascended Master Morya who was embodied as Melzone, one of the chief Magi and as the patriarch Abraham; Abraham was considered in Judaic thought during the period of Jesus' lifetime as being in Heaven, hence the familiar phrase "in the bosom of Father Abraham." Therefore, it seems that he either was a living master or an Ascended Being incarnating during Jesus' lifetime as

Melzone (Melchior); or, as it is generally thought, that he postponed his Ascension until later to further develop humanity's acceptance of the teachings. Esoterically known as Morya Melzone.

Mother God - Our Mother, a person of the Trinity; Visel; Sophia of the Gnostics; the Goddess Wisdom; Wisdom; The Holy Breath; The Holy Spirit; Truth. See Visel; Holy Spirit; Sophia.

Nada - (nah - duh) - "generous"; "giving"; "voice of the silence (Nirvana)." Ascended Lady Master Nada, who embodied as Miriam, the Prophetess, the sister of Moses and later as Miriam, the kindred soul of Jesus.
She was known as Mary (Maria or Miriam) the Jewess, the famous alchemist in Egypt, who invented the still and the bain-marie or double boiler. She founded many communities devoted to the Christine Gnosis (early Gnosticism) in Egypt. Nada has been confounded and confused with Mary Magdalene. See Magdala; Mary Magdalene.

Nazarene - Epithet of Jesus referring to him hailing from Nazareth.

Nazarite - "consecrated to God." Ascetic in ancient Judaism; John the Baptist (Elijah) was a Nazarite and was known as the Brother Nazarite by the Silent Brotherhood and simply as the Nazarite by the Christines. See Elijah.

Neptune - The name Neptune is related to the name of the Hindu and Zoroastrian god Apam Napat meaning "child of the waters", who was said to be the fire god who comes out of the waters; also known as Poseidon; known as the Cherubim Rama (Rama'sa) the ruler of Pisces (and the Piscean Age) and Hierarch of the Spirits of Water and Wave. He is an Aspect of the Maitreya. See Maitreya

Ormazd (ore - mahst) - Modern rendering of Ahura Mazda (Sanat Kumara); known as Oromasdes in ancient Greek and during the Middle Ages. See Ahura Mazda; Oromasis; Sanat Kumara.

Oromasis - Hierarch of the spirits of fire; Vuhori, the Cherubim of Sagittarius who manifested as Enoch the Christ and Lord Zarathustra; he is given the name Oromasis in recognition of him being the Manifest of Ahura Mazda or Ormazd.

Parabrahm - "Supremely Great Being." The Father God; Jehovah; Zeus; Thoth. See Father God.
Paradise - Area of the Realm of Soul that is of the blessed; the Kingdom of the Soul; distinct from the Purifying Fires (Purgatory); Eden. See Realms; Heaven.

Pink - Soft, light pink is a sacred color that represents maternal love, but yellow and gold better represent the Love that is Christ, which is higher; with regard to sacredness, the color of soft, light pink must ascend in vibration into lavender and then unto purples; hot pink, scarlet, fuchsia are negative; peach represents the flesh and the lower self. See Lavender.

Piscean Age - The previous 2,000 year epoch of the Christian dispensation, typified by Water Baptism, the miracle of the loaves and fishes, and the monogram of Ichthys as a symbol of Jesus Christ and of Christians. See Aquarian Age.

Planes - (1) The seven different segments of Creation, each created and ruled by the Septonate. They are in descending order Cherubim/Seraphim, Angels, Man, Animals, Plants, Earth (including elementals) and Protoplast. (2) Different levels of existence of everything that always consist of ether, spirit, matter and energy called Realms. See Realms.

Pleiades - Constellation that is a focus of the Elohim Cyclopea. In the Bible the Pleiades are associated with great and sweet blessings. In the year 2000 A.D. the constellation of the Pleiades moved from being considered within the constellation of Taurus into the constellation of Gemini, this Sign in the heavens marks the revelation of Astrochristology and the alignment of the zodiac constellations with the months of the Christian calendar and heralds the Age of Aquarius in accordance with the teaching of the *AG*. See Astrochristology.

Prince of Angels - Archangel Michael.

Prince of Fire - Oromasis. See Oromasis.

Prince of Peace - Title given to Lord Jesus and unto Melchisedec (Lord Maitreya), as representatives of the Elohim of Peace.

Purifying Fires (Purgatory) - part of the Realm of Soul where departed spirits go to be purified in the fires of the Father God and the Holy Breath, but outside and away from the Kingdom of the Soul or Paradise (Eden); unfortunately those who have so much evil and negativity within their soul may have their soul destroyed known as "the Second Death" or "being thrown into the lake of fire"; this process leaves only ones Spirit which is always Divine, but the personality and experiences of the individual are wiped away and perhaps much wisdom that had been learned; "the Second Death" will usually compel the Spirit to take a new soul and to embody again, thus starting the whole, long process over again, because the previous soul learned nothing. See Realms.

Purple - A sacred color; the Purple Ray bestows the gift of Peace and Tranquility; the Purple Flame is the Grace of God that also bestows peace and tranquility, associated with Ascension process; it is an aspect of the Violet

Flame, which dissolves karma and all negativity. See Gold; Fire Baptism.

Quan Yin - "one who hears the cries of the world." The Buddhist and Taoist name for the Seraphim Akmaquil (s' Akmaquil); the Buddhist and Taoist Goddess of Mercy; a Demigod known as the Goddess of Mercy; Aquaria; the Seraphim of Aquarius; Co-Ruler of the Age of Aquarius; usually depicted carrying a vase containing the Waters of Immortality.

Realms - Different levels of existence that always consist of ether, spirit, matter and energy; they are: (1) the Realm of Spirit - Akasha, Kingdom of Heaven, High Heaven, the highest heaven or plane, the fastest vibrations of ether, spirit, matter and energy; (2) the Realm of Soul - Paradise and the Purifying Fires, lower, slower, thicker vibrations; (3) the Realm of Manifest or the Plane of Manifest - Hell and Limbo, the World of our current existence, illusion, the lowest, slowest, thickest vibrations of ether, spirit, matter and energy; the only realm where evil can truly be experienced, our school.

Rolls of Graphael - Akashic Records, the Book of Life. See Akasha; Akashic Records; Graphael.

Sacred Colors - See Aqua, Blue, Fire Baptism, Gold, Green, Indigo, Lavender, Pink, Purple, Veronica, Violet,

White, Yellow.

Saint Germain - "holy brother." Joseph the Essene, father of Jesus, a carpenter by trade; Ascended Master Saint Germain; embodied earlier as the prophet Samuel; and later as the living Ascended Master known as the mysterious wonder-worker, the Count of Saint Germain; he founded many Masonic and Rosicrucian lodges; Saint Germain is the bearer of the Violet Flame of Transformation unto mankind for their Eternal Freedom, which is the Ascension Process. See Violet.

Sananda - "joy." Hindu name for the Aspect of the Elohim Orion for the earth and our solar system. Mighty Victory is the Cherubic Aspect of Sananda and Jesus the Christ was the Manifest of Love, the Elohim of Love, who is Sananda.

Sanat Kumara - (saw - not - coo - mar - ruh) "eternal youth." Hindu name for Ahura Mazda, the Aspect of Elohim Arcturus for the earth and our solar system. See Ahura Mazda.

Septonate - The Elohim, the Seven Spirits before the throne of God that performed the act of creation and created mankind - male and female, in their image. They are known as the Elohim and the Lesser Gods in the *AG*. See Elohim; Lesser Gods.

Serapis - (sarah) Another name for Osiris; Ascended Master Serapis; Grasgarben, the Cherubim of Libra who manifested as Manetho and Matheno; known as Serapis Bey, which means the Seraphic Lord, which refers to him working closely with the Seraphim. See Manetho.

Sevenfold Flame - The Sacred Flame of the Seven Mighty Elohim, it is sevenfold and rests above one's eyebrows like a crown; it is most often a Sevenfold Golden Flame, but can be any sacred color and is often all of the sacred colors. See Fire Baptism.

Seven Sages - A college of Seven of the most evolved metaphysical masters in the world that meets at the dawning of each Cosmic Age; they formulated the Seven Postulates; Ashbina and Philo were Sages, the other five are Ascended Masters. See Apollo; Djwal Kul; Divine Director; Lanto; Maha Chohan; Manu; Mencius; Morya; Serapis.

Silence, the Great - Nirvana; the Realm of Spirit; Heaven. See Realms.

Silent Brotherhood (Clothed in Shimmering White) - A supernatural college of ascended masters who are clothed in shimmering white who are able to go back and forth between the different Realms of existence; heavenly beings who have become one with their Divine

Self and can appear to humans on this plane. Identical to the Great White Brotherhood. See Great White Brotherhood.

Sophia - "wisdom." The Gnostic name for the Mother God, the Holy Breath (Spirit).

Surya - "God's Command." The Elohim of Sirius and an Aspect of the Elohim Hercules, who came to our world to Manifest the Cosmic Christ, the Maitreya for our earth, establish the Melchisedec Priesthood and pave the way for the ministry of Jesus the Christ. See Maitreya.

Tao - (dow) "the Way." The Chinese term for Brahm, the I AM, the Universal Breath (Spirit), God.

Thoth - (thought) "he who balances." Egyptian name for the Father God.

Triune God - The Trinity. God the Father, the Mother and Christ the Son; Father, Son and Holy Spirit.

Veronica - "true image." A sacred icon revealing and mirroring one's true self.; a visual image of a great Pillar of Light (Pillar of Cloud) which is the Immersion in Light, with one's True Self which is Divine Spirit (I AM Spirit, the Higher Self) at the top; the Holy Christ Self or Soul that has found the Christ in the middle (sometimes without this pictured, but still understood to be there) ; and the physical body enveloped in the Violet Flame representing the Temple of the Indwelling Holy Spirit and the Baptism by Fire. See I AM; I AM Spirit; Jahhevahe.

Violet - A sacred color; the Violet Flame is the mercy of God which dissolves karma and negativity within the individual's physical body and the soul.

Visel - (viz - ell, not like 'chisel') "Energy of God"; "God of the Expanse"; "Wise God." Related to the word 'wise,' similarly in Sanskrit the word 'vidya' meaning wisdom. The phoneme 'vis' conveys several meanings, such as: energy; wisdom; expanse; and vision; The Mother God, the Holy Breath, the Goddess Wisdom. See Holy Spirit; Mother God.

White - A sacred color that represents Purity and Hope; the Pillar of Light that is used in visualizing the Immersion in Light, is white vibrating almost blue; the White Flame purifies the individual and the atmosphere.

Wisdom, the Goddess Wisdom - (1) Visel, the Mother God. See Holy Breath, Holy Spirit, Mother God, Visel. (2) Virtue of intelligence and discernment.

Yellow - A sacred color which represents the Wisdom that is Christ, and that comes from the Mother God, as does the color gold. See Gold.

Zeus - "to shine"; "sky"; "God." Greek name of the Father God; Jehovah; Parabrahm; Thoth. See Father God.

Zoroaster - (Zorro - aster) "golden star." Greek form of Zarathustra. See Oromasis.

Passages from the Holy Bible Index

John 10: 34 ... V
John 16: 13 ... IV

1st John 4: 16 ... V

Revelation 1: 4 ... VI
Revelation 5: 6 ... VI

Notes

[1] Encyclopedic Theosophical Glossary.

[2] A.D.K. Luk, "Law of Life, Book II," Pg. 295.

[3] Saint Germain, "Ascended Master Instruction, Vol. IV," Pg. 45.
[4] Eliphas Levi, "Rituel Et Dogme de La Haute Magie."

[5] A.D.K. Luk, "The Law of Life and Teachings of Divine Beings, Book I ," Pp. 62-65.

[6] Mark Booth, "The Secret History of the World," Pg. 146.

[7] Encyclopedic Theosophical Glossary.

[8] A.D.K. Luk, "The Law of Life, Book II," Pg. 291.

[9] Gustav Davidson, "A Dictionary of Angels," Pg. 125.
[10] A.D.K. Luk, "The Law of Life, Book II," Pg. 291.

[11] Gustav Davidson, "A Dictionary of Angels," Pg. 30

[12] H. Spencer Lewis, "The Mystical Life of Jesus," Pg. 188.

[13] Mark Booth, "The Secret History of the World," Pg. 146.

[14] A.D.K. Luk, "The Life & Teachings of Jesus & Mary," Pg. 44.

[15] Mark L. Prophet & Elizabeth Clare Prophet, "The Masters & Their Retreats," Pg. 54.

[16] Ibid., Pg. 143.

[17] H. Spencer Lewis, "The Mystical Life of Jesus," Pp. 80, 121-122.

[18] Ibid., Pg. 213

[19] Gustav Davidson, "A Dictionary of Angels," Pg. 324.

[20] A.D.K. Luk, "The Law of Life, Book II," Pg. 255.

[21] H. Spencer Lewis, "The Mystical Life of Jesus," Pg. 83.
[22] Ibid., Pg. 80.

[23] Ibid., Pg. 84; A.D.K. Luk, "The Law of Life, Book II," Pg. 274.

[24] H. Spencer Lewis, "The Mystical Life of Jesus," Pg. 81.

[25] A.D.K. Luk, "The Law of Life, Book II," Pg. 260.

[26] A.D.K. Luk, "The Life & Teachings of Jesus & Mary," Pg. 16.

[27] A.D.K. Luk, "The Law of Life, Book II," Pg. 292.

[28] H. Spencer Lewis, "The Mystical Life of Jesus," Pg. 131.

[29] A.D.K. Luk, "The Life & Teachings of Jesus & Mary," Pg. 63.

[30] A.D.K. Luk, "The Law of Life, Book II," Pp. 272-273.

[31] H. Spencer Lewis, "The Mystical Life of Jesus," Pg. 84.

[32] Mark L. Prophet & Elizabeth Clare Prophet, "The Masters & Their Retreats," Pg. 333-334.
[33] A.D.K. Luk, "The Life & Teachings of Jesus & Mary;" H. Spencer Lewis, "The Mystical Life of Jesus."

[34] Mark Booth, "The Secret History of the World," Pg. 361-362.

[35] Mark L. Prophet & Elizabeth Clare Prophet, "The Masters & Their Retreats," Pg. 54.

[36] A.D.K. Luk, "The Law of Life, Book II," Pg. 291.

[37] Eliphas Levi, "Rituel Et Dogme de La Haute Magie."

[38] A.D.K. Luk, "The Law of Life, Book II," Pg. 275.

[39] Mark Booth, "The Secret History of the World," Pg. 360-362.

[40] Harriette Augusta Curtiss & F. Homer Curtiss, "The Message of Aquaria," Pg. viii.

Acknowledgments & Suggested Reading

"A Dictionary of Angels," Gustav Davidson. The Free Press, Macmillan, Inc., New York, New York. (1967)

"Ascended Master Instruction, Vol. IV," Saint Germain. Saint Germain Press, Schaumburg, Illinois. (1986)

"Biopneuma: The Science of the Great Breath," Levi H. Dowling. (1921)

"Encyclopedic Theosophical Glossary," G. de Purucker, Editor- in-Chief. Theosophical University Press Online. (1999)

"Jesus Christ, Leader of Men," Swami Abhedananda.

"Keys to the Kingdom," Elizabeth Clare Prophet. Summit University Press.

"Rituel Et Dogme de La Haute Magie," Eliphas Levi.

"Self Culture," Levi H. Dowling. (1921)

"The Aquarian Gospel of Jesus the Christ," Levi H. Dowling. DeVorss & Co., Marina del Rey, California. (1907)

"The Law of Life, Books I & II," A.D.K. Luk. A.D.K. Luk Publications, Pueblo, Colorado. (1960)
"The Law of Life & Teachings of Divine Beings, Book I," A.D.K. Luk. A.D.K. Luk Publications, Pueblo, Colorado. (1978)

"The Life and Teachings of Jesus and Mary," A.D.K. Luk. A.D.K. Luk Publications, Pueblo, Colorado. (1966)

"The Life of Saint Issa," Nicholas Notovich.

"The Lost Years of Jesus," Elizabeth Clare Prophet. Summit Univerity Press, Livingston, Montana. (1987).

"The Masters & Their Retreats," Mark L. Prophet & Elizabeth Clare Prophet. Summit University Press. (2003)

"The Message of Aquaria," Harriette Augusta Curtiss & F. Homer Curtiss. The Curtiss Philosophic Book Co., San Francisco, California; J.F. Rowny Press, Los Angeles, California. (1923)

"The Mystical Life of Jesus," H. Spencer Lewis. The Grand Lodge of the English Language Jurisdiction, the

Ancient & Mystical Order Rosae Crucis, Inc., U.S. A.. (1929)

"The New English Bible." The Delegates of the Oxford University Press & the Syndics of the Cambridge University Press, U.K.. (1961)

"The Secret History of the World," Mark Booth. The Overlook Press, Peter Mayer Publishers, Inc., Woodstock & New York, New York. (2008)

"Twelve Lessons in Truth - Aum," Julianna McKee. J.F. Rowny Press, Los Angeles, California. (1931)

Lynne in NS

7940 Bodega Ave.
Apt 3
Sebastopol CA 95472

LaVergne, TN USA
15 August 2010
193409LV00002B/160/P